Brian Hennigan's
Scottish Urban Myths

Brian Hennigan was born and raised in Scotland, although his business career spans many industries and countries. His fiction has been broadcast on BBC Radio Four and Radio Scotland and his first novel, *Patrick Robertson – A Tale of Adventure*, was selected by Ian Rankin as one of the Books of the Year in *The Sunday Telegraph*.

Also by Brian Hennigan

Patrick Robertson – A Tale of Adventure

Brian Hennigan's
Scottish Urban Myths

BLACK & WHITE PUBLISHING

First published 2002
by Black & White Publishing Ltd
99 Giles Street, Edinburgh EH6 6BZ

ISBN 1 902927 27 3

A CIP catalogue record for this book
is available from The British Library.

Typeset by Hewer Text Ltd, Edinburgh
Printed and bound by Omnia Books Ltd, Bishopbriggs

For Bill and Margaret Hennigan

Contents

Important Introduction

'Gather round, and let me tell you compact tales of wonder, the likes of which will warm the ear lobes more cheerily than your favourite balaclava.'

How many of us have heard these words in bus-shelters all over the land as the kindly old Scotch storyteller approaches, offering pithy tales in exchange for a 'lucky dip' in our polythene bag of shopping? Minutes later, as the elderly man stumbles beerily homeward with an exciting assortment of tinned goods, we are able to endure the remaining wait more thoughtfully than before.

Yet gifted though such storytellers may be, even they would not claim to have crafted these deliciously short stories. Their role is simply to relay, to distribute, acting as the gabbling conduit whereby the mini-legends zoom mysteriously around our collective consciousness.

So where do these tales, these urban myths come from? They are as near to a universal in storytelling as can be imagined, with evidence of their genesis to be found in hieroglyphic etchings in Egypt, primitive cave paintings in France, and convenience-store felt-tip scrawls in Prestonpans. They are in many respects an eternal panacea for tired minds, the bite-size antidote to the drudgery of life, BC or AD, a.m. or p.m. For despite their apparent modern pedigree, none of these tales has been made up at any recent time. They are, in fact, amalgams of tales from

Greece, ancient Rome and the mysterious lands to the East, including Bathgate. And ancient though their heritage might be, the need for story-based relaxation has never been greater. In a world where the random appears the norm, such stories, through their simple structure, remind our souls of the importance of order.

Yet it would be wrong to imply that these fables are without harmful effect. In contemporary life the telling and re-telling of urban myths has come to dominate most social, and much business conversation. Not since the Black Plague has a virus spread with such devastating effect. Productivity has suffered, scholarship decreased. Even birth rates have declined as couples, distracted from their traditional bedtime activity, thrill each other with pillow-gripping story after story of something that happened to a friend of a friend.

Nevertheless, the overwhelming moral of these tales is that – to follow Aristotle – people get what is coming to them. Dance though they may in the jolly headlight beam of life, few can avoid the oncoming car of fate.

So read my selection of Scottish urban myths with one eye looking over your shoulder and the other on the open road. Remember that it is because every tale is, more or less, anonymous that the subject of each is never in doubt.

There but for the grace of a narrative-driven God go you.

Brian Hennigan
Buenos Aires, 2002

Vital Acknowledgements

Compiling this book took many years of research, travelling the glens, highways and chip shops of the land. Much time was spent in shopping centres, out of town furniture warehouses and doctors' waiting-rooms, coaxing the good people of Scotland into grudging conversation. A word here, a word there and gradually a composite tale is formed.

From depot to terminus and station to station, the Scottish public transport systems have proven invaluable. I owe each and every one a debt of appreciation. The nation's bed and breakfasts played their part, providing succour and toast after many a day on the open road with nothing but a kagoul and a half-bottle of Famous Grouse for company.

Scottish pubs proved invaluable in mining my way to the golden core of much of the material herein. Asking questions – particularly too many questions – can be dangerous, and to those who were there on that night in Dufftown, my thanks for your protection.

Certain individuals went out of their way to provide assistance, offering handwritten versions when others were fearful of the potential repercussions of putting inkjet to paper. To these dedicated few: Catherine Cooper, James Hardie, Donna Krachan, Charlie Maclean, Rowena Jeffreys-Jones and Graham Thomas – I owe a particular spoon of gratitude.

Brian Hennigan's
Scottish Urban Myths

East Lothian Truth Machine

A spate of minor thefts in and around North Berwick were causing the police much consternation. The townsfolk were increasingly annoyed at the vanishing of all-weather furniture items from their manicured lawns, and there was talk of little else on the shuttle trains to and from Edinburgh.

Sending one of their best men undercover, the constabulary were able to infiltrate the horticultural underworld and, in so doing, soon established the identity of a suspect. Yet for all that they were confident of his identity and guilt, there was little evidence to connect him to the crimes. Furthermore, a limited budget meant that a comprehensive surveillance operation was out of the question.

The crunch came when a member of the town council had two of their most valuable gnomes removed from their garden in the dead of the night. The word went out that the suspect had to be taken into custody and a confession obtained. Bringing the man to their station in the wee small hours, the arresting officers were dismayed to discover that, dim though their subject was, he was also nevertheless unwilling to admit anything, and adamant about his innocence.

The senior officer then had an idea. The suspect was asked if he would be prepared to make his statements while attached to a lie detector. When he agreed, the man found himself taken into another room. Here the officers had rigged up a photocopier attached by crocodile clips to a metal colander, which was placed on the suspect's head. From then on, to each of the man's statements an officer would punch a button, producing a pre-prepared printed sheet with the words 'HE'S LYING'. After a mere five minutes of questioning, and seeing the evidence building up against him, the man confessed. Only one of the gnomes was recovered.

It Could be You

A gloomy Forfar Christmas. The sales director of an engineering firm was treating his staff to a seasonal dinner of diminutive extravagance. There was no Santa Claus, and a raffle was held to decide who got to pull the cracker. When their boss went away to have a drink with some golf club chums at the bar, his over-worked team finished off the cheap house wine and decided to play a wee joke. Quickly looking through his suit jacket, they found the sales director's ticket for the National Lottery. Calling the waitress over, they handed her a copy of the numbers.

Fifteen minutes later the boss was back, urging everyone to 'go wild' over the lethargic-looking Death by Chocolate. Then the waitress appeared.

'Would anyone like to know tonight's winning Lottery numbers?'

Everyone nodded. As each of the team checked their own tickets, a look of befuddled delight began to creep across their boss's face. With a trembling paw he reached into his jacket, pulling out his Lottery ticket with evident awe. Then he asked the waitress to say the numbers again. As she reached the last one, it became too much. Jumping up, the sales director grabbed the paper from her hand, compared the numbers with those on his ticket, and began jigging round the table. Before anyone could stop him, he stopped himself, standing behind his secretary,

Fiona. Placing his hand on her shoulder, he addressed the room.

'You can have no idea how much I despise working here. If it weren't for Fiona, with whom I have been having an affair for the past three years, I'd have left years ago. As it is, I can leave now. You and all the tossers from the golf club can go to hell. And you can take my sweaty wife with you. Fiona – I'll meet you in the car park.'

It was some time after his team finished theirs, that anyone bothered to tell their boss about his own just desserts.

Press 'Return'

Early one morning a Chicago employee of one of the world's largest software companies received a telephone call from a distressed man with a Scottish accent. The conversation was recorded.

'Technical desk. How may I help?'

'Hello, this is Jim. I'm calling from Stirling.'

'OK, Jim. Take your time. How can I help?'

'Well, I'm having trouble with your programme.'

'What sort of trouble, sir?'

'It's terrible. I was just typing along and all of a sudden the words went away.'

'Went away?'

'They disappeared. I looked round the back but they're not there either.'

'OK. So what does your screen look like now, sir?'

'Nothing'.

'Nothing?'

'It's blank. It won't do anything.'

'Are you still in our programme, sir, or did you get out?'

'How do I tell?'

'Well, can you see the programme window on the screen?'

'What's a programme window? Janice never told me about them.'

'Who's Janice?'

'The nice wee lassie in the computer shop.'

'Fine. Tell me, sir, can you move the cursor around on the screen?'

'There isn't any cursor. I told you, it won't accept anything I type.'

'Does your monitor have a "power on" indicator?'

'What's a monitor?'

'It's the thing on your desk that looks like a TV.'

'We invented them.'

'Invented what, sir?'

'TVs. We invented them. John Logie Baird.'

'OK, well do you see the TV-like thing? That's a monitor. Now, does it have a little light that tells you when it's on?'

'I don't know.'

'Can you please look on the back of the monitor and see where the mains lead goes into it. Can you see that?'

'Yes, I think so.'

'Great. Follow the cable to the plug and tell me if it's plugged into the wall.'

'Hold on a wee minute . . . yes it is.'

'When you were behind the monitor, did you notice that there were two cables plugged into the back of it, not just one?'

'No.'

'Well, there are. I'd like you to look again and find the other cable.'

'Right, I've found it.'

'Follow it for me, and tell me if it's plugged securely into the back of your computer.'

'I can't reach.'

'Can you see if it is?'

'No, it's too dark.'

'Too dark?'

'Yes, all the lights are out.'

'Well then, turn them on.'

'I can't. We're having a power cut.'

'A power . . . a power cut? Okay, we've got it sorted now, sir. Do you still have the boxes and manuals and packing that your computer came in?'

'Yes, I keep them in the cupboard. Next to the rubbish bags.'

'Good. Go and get them, then unplug your system and pack it up just like it was when you bought it. Then take it back to Janice in the shop you bought it from.'

'Really? Is it that bad?'

'Yes, I'm afraid it is.'

'Oh dear. What do I tell Janice when I take it back?'

'Just tell her you're too stupid to own a computer.'

Bad Vibes

The ghost tours of old Edinburgh are renowned for their chilling authenticity, as first-year students jump out on weary bands of foreign tourists. As the tours wind their money-making way around the labyrinthine back passages of the capital, there is ample time for the international visitor to gasp at the layer upon layer of history that has formed the town's proud heritage. That this journey into history is continually interrupted by the not-quite scary tones of a caped 23-year-old from London inviting everyone to 'watch out for the poltergeist' is to be regretted – if not altogether condemned.

On one such tour the atmosphere throughout had been completely cold. Thanks to the universal presence of Sean Connery, most visitors know what a Scottish accent should sound like and their group leader, fresh from a home visit to Bury St Edmonds, didn't have one. Having put up with all manner of unlikely executions, assaults and robberies, the majority of the visitors were keen for a return to the hotel. Yet on entering a particularly fore-boding stoned courtyard, there was a rare thespian treat. No sooner had the tour come to a halt in front of an old wooden door, than there arose a truly terrifying scream from nearby.

Turning, those at the back were pleased to see the arrival of a demonic-looking woman, wielding an enormous wooden stake. Still screaming, this harridan ran through the gleeful crowd and plunged the stake repeatedly into the body of the astonished-looking group leader, whose acting had taken an unexpected turn for the better. There was spontaneous applause.

It was several minutes later, while all the time their leader lay twitching and moaning on the ground in a lather of blood and flesh, that some in the group began to wonder whether something was up.

The murderer was eventually traced to an apartment overlooking the stone courtyard. Having listened to the ghost tour's melodramatic tones welling up through her window for over ten years, the woman had cracked and decided to stop their visitations once and for all. A plaque commemorating the sacrifice of the group leader in the service of tourism can still be seen.

Multiple Deposits

Greenock crooks are notoriously clever, shaming the rest of the Scottish underworld with their intelligent, analysis-based approach to bad deeds. A prince among these clever criminals adopted a most perceptive way of getting money out of financial institutions.

Wandering unnoticed into a high street bank in Glasgow, the man picked up a large handful of deposit slips. Taking these home, he used a specially adapted laser printer with an illegally obtained magnetic ink to fill in his own bank account number at the bottom of each blank form. He then returned these customised slips to the same bank. The result was that each time one of these slips was processed through the bank's automated systems, the computer read the criminal's account number in preference to the customer's. By the end of one week, several hundred thousand pounds had been accumulated. The money was then withdrawn and the account closed, leaving the bank to hush up how they had been duped to the tune of a lot of other peoples' pounds.

Beef Wellington

One chilly January morning the bedraggled crew of a Western Isles fishing boat were found in the Sound of Sleat, clinging terrier-like to the wreck of their boat. Following their rescue, and after due care had been applied, the authorities set about establishing what had happened. To a man, every member of the five-man crew insisted that the boat had been sunk after a cow, appearing out of a clear blue sky, had struck the fishing vessel amidships, shattering its hull and sinking the boat in a matter of minutes.

Suspecting that this story was some sort of cover-up for bad seamanship, the captain was arrested while investigations continued. Rumours began to circulate concerning the lifestyle of those concerned, with allegations of all-day drinking sprees on the waves being made. The children of the crew were taunted at school by friends swooping by them going, 'Moo!'

Yet one day the Russian Air Force informed the Scottish authorities that the air crew of one of its cargo planes had been caught running a contraband meat-smuggling operation. The large green plane would land at outlying farms on the Russian steppes, capture a number of cows, then fly them to a rendez-vous with Russian Mafia middle-men, who would then sell the precious meat on to Moscow restaurants. Two weeks previously the gang, having been tracked by radar, were intercepted over Russian airspace and ordered to land. Defying these instructions, the bulky plane attempted to escape, making its way towards the UK. Eager apparently to hide any evidence of illegal activity, they jettisoned their cargo of cows 'somewhere over Scotland', before landing in Ireland and claiming political asylum. Individually interrogated by the Irish police, one of the Russians broke down, revealing the truth and ensuring their swift, involuntary return to their homeland and a court martial. No cows were ever recovered.

Aberdonian Conversion

A powerful, unmarried businesswoman from Aberdeen was notoriously ungenerous when it came to Christmas. She begrudged all her staff their festive holidays and resented the need to offer any form of seasonal bonus. There came a time, though, when this single, successful tycoon experienced a form of epiphany.

On a late December business trip to far-flung Glasgow, she was overwhelmed by the chummy, all-embracing generosity of those she met. Standing on Sauchiehall Street – her mind released by several large whiskies – she resolved to become a better, more giving person. Aware of the twinkling fairy lights above her, she also resolved that the change would come about that very Christmas.

Returning to her North-East home, the woman ordered a set of deluxe greeting cards. As the next day was the last before the Christmas holidays began, there was no time for her to go shopping for gifts for all her staff. Still wishing to demonstrate her newly born warmth, she wrote out a cheque from her own personal account to each and every one of them. Then she addressed and signed all of the envelopes.

With dawn approaching, the fresh-spirited but weary-brained businesswoman crawled into bed. But following the return to work in the New Year, she was a little perplexed that no one offered any thanks for their presents. Indeed, if anything, the atmosphere in the company seemed to be even more frosty than usual.

Taking her secretary aside, the business magnate asked for an explanation.

'It was the cards,' was as much as she could get out of the tight-lipped underling.

Returning that night to her expensive home, the woman decided to open a bottle of wine to cheer herself up. Opening the dining-room drawer she was stunned to discover the pile of cheques she had written – and then forgotten to stick in all of the Christmas cards. The same Christmas cards that had a personal note advising, 'I wish you a Merry Christmas. Sorry, but you'll have to buy your own present this year!'

Silent Departure

A newspaper house in Glasgow was stunned by the unexpected death of one of its longest serving proof-readers. Old Jimmy had been with the company for more than 40 years when he was discovered at his desk one Thursday afternoon. The postmortem revealed that he had been dead for about four days.

When asked why no one seemed to have noticed, the section manager explained,

'Everyone keeps themselves to themselves round here. Jimmy seemed a bit down but we just thought that was because of the football result on the Saturday. He's been like that before. It's a pity because he was always a popular, polite old guy. Everyone liked him.'

Following this incident a new procedure was introduced whereby a loud bell is rung every day at five o'clock. All staff failing to respond are given a quick twist of the ear by the responsible supervisor.

Tobermory Popeye

The effect of the mass media on the people of Tobermory is a matter of legend. One case illustrates the phenomenon in the extreme. Cartoons were always one of the most decisive imports to the island capital's culture and none more so than the weekly stories of *Popeye*. Every week the town's children folk would huddle round the television set, awaiting the latest adventures of the muscular sailor. A small boy on the north side of town was particularly smitten, even demanding that his mother provide him with tinned spinach – the character's own strength-inspiring dish – at every meal.

This apparently comical tale of obsession took a nasty turn when the mother was out at a friend's house on a gloomy Friday. Realising his opportunity, the youngster broke into the locked store of tins and consumed every one he could find. He died three days later in a mainland hospital, the victim of a rare case of spinach poisoning.

Man's Best Friend

For several years high street banks on the West Coast were troubled by the Scotty Dog Shaker. On a slow Tuesday morning a man in a brown Balaclava and dark sunglasses walked into one bank's main branch in Oban holding a white West Highland Terrier. Thrusting the dog up against the window of a concerned teller, the man explained that, unless he received £250 immediately, he would 'hurt the wee doggie'. The stunned cashier refused to do anything, at which point the man began shaking the little dog with escalating prejudice. Startled, the woman employee grabbed a handful of twenty pound notes and stuffed them through the window, whereupon the man grabbed them and left. The bank, although alarmed, did not wish it to be known that they had been robbed by a man armed only with a small dog, and did not pursue the matter with either the police or their insurance company. The money was written off as a 'cash machine error'.

As the months went by it soon became clear that this was no one-off incident, as rumours spread among bank staff. Eventually a group of senior managers from the different banks contacted the police to explain what had been happening. After consultation with the RSPCA, a notice was issued to all employees that no further cash was to be paid out, regardless of how much the man shook the dog, the advice being that the terrier would probably turn on its owner before substantial damage occurred. In Portree one week later the masked man and dog appeared at a well-informed teller's window, who refused resolutely to hand over any money. As the shaking of the dog became more pronounced, a housewife – who was setting up an account for her children – ran outside, got the £250 out of the ATM and gave it to the newly-unnerved man. Upon receiving this, he handed her the dog, saying, 'His name is Hugh and he doesn't like loud music,' before running from the premises. No further incidents have been reported.

Galashiels Cinema Life

Weddings in Galashiels are famed nationwide for the timeless element that the hosts always strive to install in the ceremony. One couple from the town was determined that theirs should be an occasion of Hollywood proportions. They had met when their hands touched at the local video store, both reaching for the same copy of Kevin Costner's *Robin Hood – Prince of Thieves*.

For the wedding, both were united in wishing to capture that moment for eternity. It was therefore decided to have the organist play the romantic theme music 'Everything I Do, I Do It For You' – made famous by Canadian songster Bryan Adams – as the bride walked down the aisle. Consulting with both priest and organ player, there seemed to be no problem with this request, although the latter seemed a little taken aback by the choice of music.

Come the day and all the arrangements fell into place. The bride looked resplendent in peach satin, the groom most handsome in a kilt woven from the distinctive tartan of Galashiels Rugby Football Club. As the doors of the off-white Mercedes closed, the organist struck up, beginning the music with a swelling intro.

Unfortunately, it turned out that the elderly organist was not familiar with the Kevin Costner version of the tale of Robin Hood. His understanding of what was required was based on the '60s television series. So it was that the Borders bride marched tearfully towards her embarrassed husband-to-be as the congregation began to sing, 'Robin Hood, Robin Hood, riding through the glen. Robin Hood, Robin Hood and his band of men.'

Laughing Stock

A man from Edinburgh had a cat, Fat Gregory, who was his sole companion, a gargantuan beast which worried most of the neighbourhood dogs and for whom the man had built a special outsized entrance. Living in a small house near the centre of town was convenient, although during the famous Edinburgh Festival, it could be a bit noisy. This did not trouble the man too much. On most nights after work he would go forthwith to the pub, passing the evening with his drinking chums until stumbling home at all hours to feed Fat Gregory and go to bed.

One sunny August, midway through the famous Edinburgh Festival, the man came home at around one o'clock in the morning. Tripping his way up to the front door, it was then he realised that he had locked himself out. From inside he could hear Fat Gregory miaowing for his food. Unable to remember who he kept a spare set of keys with, the man bent over and, with a degree of optimism common to those filled end to end with beer, attempted to enter the house through the cat-flap. Having managed to get his head and one shoulder through, the man found himself stuck. Pitifully he began wailing himself, creating a terrible union of misery with the hungry cries of Fat Gregory.

Two passing theatre performers, returning from their own show at one of the smaller Edinburgh Festival venues, spotted the figure of the man. Themselves some-what tipsy, they took advantage of the poor unfortunate, even as he lay struggling on his knees. Pulling down his trousers, they set about painting his posterior into a landscape featuring Edinburgh Castle – a white cane from the garden serving as an impolitely placed flagpole, complete with a small Scottish flag.

It was fully twenty-four hours before the man was rescued from this distressing position. Until then, all passers-by mistook the scene for a piece of student street theatre. Indeed, the man made over £150 from donations.

Ullapool Revelation

Rural Scotland is not designed for meeting the right partner. The distances are long and the road is seldom straight. Opportunities to meet new and interesting members of any, let alone the opposite, sex are not commonplace. Therefore the Internet has proven to be a boon for countryside romance. Lonely individuals are now able to contact each other through chat boards, meeting-rooms and other electronic artifice.

A teenage girl, having found new life through the Christmas gift of a computer of her own, was soon making all manner of contacts. Initially bashful, her communications became more adventurous and before long she had met up with someone who seemed to share many of the same interests. With her using the name Fancy Flora and him, Braveheart, they would spend hours conversing across the ether.

Gradually, their words became more and more romantic, and after that it was only a short step into the downright physical. The modems buzzed with debauched longings and wishes. With the end of her school life approaching, the newly emboldened young woman suggested a meeting at a hotel in a mutually convenient town. So it was that the two arranged to meet in Ullapool, on a dark March evening.

That night the teenager arrived at the room first.

Making full use of the complimentary miniature soaps and shampoos, Fancy Flora set about making herself resplendent for her e-mail lover. There was a tentative knock at the door.

'Come in,' suggested Flora, sitting on the edge of the invitingly large bed.

The door opened and in walked the rampant figure of Braveheart himself. Their eyes met. It was her father.

Good Catch

Saltcoats is one of the finest resorts in Scotland and attracts a variety of holidaymakers from all over parts of Glasgow. A mother and her son were one such group. Together they enjoyed a stress-free day near the sea and had soon left all the troubles of their world behind them. Sitting on the bus that night, both vowed to return, even as the automatic doors were closing on their day in paradise.

The next morning, the son complained of severe stomach ache. Even when offered some sweets, the lad would not perk up. Fearing some infection or other, the mother took him round to the nearest doctor, where the pain turned to convulsions. Alarmed, the doctor arranged for an ambulance to take both forthwith to hospital.

Sitting in the anonymous, publicly-funded building, the mother listened with a mother's concern as the sound of her son's gagging came through the curtain that the nurse and doctor had drawn across the consulting area. Eventually the nurse beckoned her to come round. There, sitting pale and tired in bed, was her son. Sitting next to him on the bedside table was a small stainless steel pan, containing dozens of tiny crabs, scuttling around.

The doctor surmised that the boy must have ingested

some crab eggs while swimming, and that they had incubated and hatched in the boy's tender stomach.

Yet even despite this episode, both mother and son continued to love Saltcoats and to visit there whenever they could.

Pet Recreation

A newly-married couple had barely settled into their swish semi-detached home in Arbroath, when the nextdoor neighbours asked if they would mind keeping an eye on their pets while they themselves were visiting friends 'down South' for the weekend. Happy to be of service, the young couple agreed, imagining that a system for the exchange of such favours would soon be in place. Besides, they liked animals, themselves being the owners of Olga, a plump mongrel bitch they had saved from the kennels. Having been educated in the various dining habits of the animals, the young couple declared themselves to be in full understanding of all diets.

On the first day of their neighbours' holiday, the couple took Olga through with them while they fed first the numerous rabbits in the pen, then the two cats and finally the goldfish in the living-room. Following this they stepped outside to take a number of Polaroid photographs of each other standing, arms by their sides, in front of their new property, these images being a request from both sets of parents. Barely had the first shot been taken, than the husband looked down to see the excited shape of Olga coming towards him, thrashing its tail and growling through a full mouth. With horror, the young man realised that Olga had the dead body of a rabbit between its teeth. Calling his wife over, together they managed to deprive the proprietorial mongrel of its catch. Picking up the motionless bunny, they noted that there was no sign of blood, merely some dirt and hair from Olga.

Making sure that there was indeed no visible external damage, they decided that the best thing to do was to pretend that nothing had happened, and to position the body in the outdoor pen as if in a state of sudden, natural death. The rabbit was duly placed to the rear of the holding on the night before the neighbours' returned. Sure enough, some few minutes after they saw the family estate car pull into its drive, the young couple received an abrupt rapping on the front door. Inviting the agitated mother and father in, they enquired about their few days away.

'Oh, that was fine,' said the father.

'The thing is,' added the mother, 'something has happened while we were away.'

Maintaining the same relaxed composure they had so rehearsed since lunchtime, the young couple enquired further.

'Well,' explained the father, 'just before we went on holiday, one of the rabbits took a funny turn and died. The children were quite upset, so we had a sort of play funeral service for the wee thing, and buried him out next to the rhubarb. When we come back, what do we find? Nothing less than that the same rabbit had at some point recovered, dug its way out of the hole, and climbed back into the pen, only to die again.'

Amazed at this story of resurrection, over the next few days the young couple watched with envy at the steady stream of visitors to the grave of the miracle bunny.

Lost at Sea

A Peterhead household, keen both to expand their knowledge of the world as well as to enjoy some of the famous 'holiday weather' they had heard of, decided to undertake a two-week tour of continental Europe. Although it was a tight fit, three generations of the northern family squeezed into their trusty Ford Granada. Mum and Dad sat in the front, while their two offspring, a boy and girl, sat either side of Granny on the back seat. Every pocket and compartment of the car was stuffed with holiday clothes and provisions, although they still ran out of sandwiches before they were halfway through Belgium. Nevertheless, they were having a good time, particularly the children.

Shortly after the French Alps, tragedy struck. Two hours after a stop for lunch, the children noticed that Granny had not said anything for some time. Giving her a pre-planned nudge from either side, both of them screamed as Granny slumped forward, thrusting her head through the front seats and coming to rest on the back of the hand brake. Father stopped immediately at the next convenient lay-by. Granny was carried out on to the grass verge where it was discovered, after a series of vigorous thumps and kicks, that she was dead.

Distraught, the children climbed back into the car, leaving Mum and Dad to consider what to do. Eventually it was agreed that it would be best to terminate the holiday. Then the question arose of what to do with the body. After much discussion, a decision was reached that Granny should be taken home with them in the car.

Starting back for Scotland, it was not long before the children in the back were complaining about having Granny next to them. Soon they were screaming, revolted to be sitting next to the stiffening corpse of their much-loved matriarch.

Stopping the car, Father got out, hauled Granny on to the boot, wrapped her in two travel blankets, and then strapped this package on to the roof-rack. Suitably calmed, the children returned to their colouring-books, as Mum and Dad plotted the route home.

Just after crossing the Dutch border on their way to the ferry, the car needed petrol. Stopping at the first Shell station they could find, the family ploughed out of the car; the father to fill-up, the mother for the bathroom, and the children for the shop. When it came to paying, Father had a terrible time with the currency, and it was several minutes before he came out again, to find the rest of his family staring at the spot where the car had been. It was never recovered, and nor was Granny. None of the four ever ate Edam again.

Grateful Dead: Paisley

Public toilets are notoriously hard to find in Paisley – a situation that causes much inconvenience for the area's many tourists. A woman from the Highlands, down on a cultural exchange weekend, was caught short after purchasing some souvenirs. Looking around, the only premises she could see were those of a funeral home.

Opening the door with great care, the highlander sneaked through the empty entrance way and into a darkened room, finding the WC behind a dark, velvet curtain. Having finished, she sought a speedy exit, only to find herself pausing, alone and reflective, in a room containing a coffin and nothing else.

To her left stood a small table with an open book. Inspection revealed this to be a book of condolence, although there were as yet no signatures therein. Feeling somewhat guilty for having used the facilities without permission, the women scribbled an entry, then left.

Two weeks later, back on Speyside, the woman received a letter from a firm of Glasgow solicitors explaining that she had inherited a substantial sum of money.

The body in the funeral hall turned out to be that of a rich old man, who, knowing his unpopularity, had left specific instructions that his money and property were to be divided between all those who bothered to turn up for his final farewell. As no one else did, the entire fortune went to the visitor from the Highlands.

Salivating Local Business People

The presence of the media in a small Scottish village is apt to produce a type of profit-driven feeding frenzy, the likes of which would make any Scot proud. The residents and shopkeepers of a quaint fishing port on the West Coast were beside themselves when word spread around that a film crew from London had that very morning arrived and booked out every room in both of the local bed and breakfasts. Everyone readied themselves for the forthcoming economic harvest.

Sure enough, by mid-morning a runner had been round most of the shops explaining the Londoner's needs and offering terms. In return for letting them stage scenes of theft, larceny and civil unrest (for a forthcoming feature on the former Yugoslavia), the producers would compensate handsomely, not only for the goods involved but also for the shopkeepers' time and the rent for two or three days of their premises. Everyone signed their release forms and by the next morning the street was seething with financial expectation.

As men with cameras positioned themselves around the town, the director's voice boomed out from a megaphone, 'OK everyone, try to look Slavic.'

Then the mayhem commenced, with stunning reality, as each shop and home was cleared of its valuables, with everything being loaded into three large white vans.

Excitedly the native population screamed to look the part, whilst giggling madly inside in anticipation of the forthcoming money.

It was almost half an hour after the last van had sped out of the village that one or two inhabitants began to wonder if the looting had not been a bit too authentic. Why, for example, had all the telephone lines been cut? And that car placed across the road to prevent access or exit?

The only beneficiary in the town from this ingenious crime was the minister, who saw a huge leap in the number of his flock, as they prayed for forgiveness and wisdom, but principally some form of compensation.

Greenock Sex Drive

Mindful that at any moment he might be chucked for want of a better postcode, a Greenock man was desperate to make a strong start with his chic Glaswegian girlfriend. With male bragging at stake, his goal was the bed and nothing else.

Sitting on the train to Central Station one day, he was alerted by a nearby conversation to the existence of foods known as 'aphrodisiacs'. Heading straight for a bookshop upon the train's arrival, he was soon the owner of a relevant manual on the subject, found in a nearby bargain bookshop called 'Hole In One'.

That evening, he worked out the type of menu that would guarantee seduction success. Being of limited resource, it was obvious that he would have to obtain the assorted asparagus, oysters, strawberries and caviar without paying for them. This was duly accomplished, with assistance from a couple of mates who were willing to help out in exchange for information from their High Priest of Love chum.

One item on the menu proved more difficult to find. The book insisted that only the freshest lobster would do, even giving instructions on how to kill one and when.

With the date set for that very night, the young Greenockian spent Saturday wandering the fishmongers of Glasgow.

Then he saw it, a beautiful red lobster paddling in a basin in a shop window of seafood dainties. Waiting until the assistants were all busy with customers, he rushed in and with one scooping movement grabbed the lobster, before running off down the street. Turning a corner and seeing an approaching police car, the young man acted with decisiveness, thrusting the animal down his trousers so that none might see.

No sooner had he done so than the snapping consequences of his actions struck. All point in hosting a romantic evening-in vanished in one painful moment, for the rest of his life.

West Lothian Bargain Mother

Shopping in Bathgate is always a treat and a young man, fresh from his job at an insurance company in Edinburgh, was enjoying himself in the supermarket. He had just deposited some baked beans in his basket when he noticed a nearby middle-aged woman looking at him, her eyes sad and pleading. The young man broke off eye contact and continued on his way, only to find that, whenever he looked up, there she was, the same woman, staring as if she knew him. This continued until he got to the check-out, where to his discomfort the woman was standing in front of him.

'Excuse me, young man,' she said in a quiet, deliberate voice.

'Yes,' he replied with trepidation.

'I must apologise for staring at you so much, but the thing is – you remind me of my only son, who died almost a year ago to this day.'

'Oh – I'm sorry,' the young man said with understanding.

'Don't be sorry,' the woman replied, 'I'm just being silly, but it's been a difficult year since then and seeing you now just reminds me how much I loved him.'

At this point the young man could feel his heart becoming heavy. Then the woman turned to him again.

'I'm sorry to ask this, but do you think you could do one wee thing for me?'

'Of course', the polite young man responded.

'Do you think that, as I leave, you could just wave to me and say, "Goodbye, Mum"?'

Pleased to be of some assistance, the young man agreed.

Two minutes later, after she had packed her groceries into five large carrier bags, the woman started for the door of the shop, turning when she was only midway there and waving. Dutifully, the young man waved back and shouted, 'Goodbye, Mum.'

A few sad minutes passed before the cashier handed the somewhat depressed young man his bill, which came to about ten times the amount he had been expecting.

'I think you've made some sort of mistake,' he said, asking the cashier to look at the receipt.

'No,' the cashier said with confidence, 'your mother said that you'd pay for all of her shopping, too.'

Pitlochry Pay-Off

The idea of something for nothing has broad appeal throughout the land. The National Lottery is for many a dream come true; the weekly, even daily opportunity to justifiably imagine getting lots of money without any effort beyond filling in some numbers – numbers which you don't even have to think of yourself.

The 26-year old unemployed man from Pitlochry who still lived with his parents could not believe his luck when, passing the television rental shop, he saw his six numbers flashing up on the screen, the same numbers he had used every week for four years. Screeching with happiness, he zoomed home, only to find that his mother had not bothered to put the numbers on for him.

His visions of rich indulgence inflated then burst in the space of half an hour, the young man took his life. It later transpired that, perhaps due to an unclean shop window, he'd been mistaken about the numbers anyway – only four of his had come up, not the required six. He had taken his life over £67.

Good Boy

An enormous bookshop in Glasgow had a young female worker who, although attractive, seemed to have little in her life other than Mungo, a large docile golden retriever. She lived alone, in what used to be her parents' house, although one of the other bookshop employees did occasionally dog-sit for Mungo, while the woman enjoyed a rare night out at the cinema, always with fellow employees.

Feeling sorry for her as another birthday loomed on the calendar, the Non-Fiction and True Crime departments – the two primary work areas for the lonely woman – got together and decided to throw a surprise party for her. The preparations got underway immediately. Firstly, a copy was made of her house keys while she was on a coffee break. Secondly, an enormous amount of party poppers, streamers and cheap good-time alcohol was bought. Thirdly, a professional photographer chum was found to document the night, in exchange for a few volumes from the Indian Cookery section, of which he was an enthusiast.

Arriving at the house before the woman returned from work, the group sat in the living-room with Mungo who, like all golden retrievers, was pleased to see them. Everyone had a beer to get into the party mood. Shortly after tea-time the front door opened and they heard the sound of the woman entering and going upstairs for a shower. Excited by the return of his mistress, Mungo made a dash for the door but was held back, then distracted by a bag of cheese and onion crisps. Meanwhile the assorted celebratory items were passed around.

Fifteen minutes later they heard the woman coming down the stairs and going into the kitchen. A few minutes passed before she called out, 'Mungo! Dinner-time.' With one burst the dog was through the door and away. Deciding that there was no point in delaying further, the gang ran through, cameras flashing and streamers flying.

'Surprise!' they shouted in unison. 'Happy Birthday!'

Arriving in the kitchen, their eyes were drawn to the sight of their young female colleague, lying on the floor, covered in crunchy peanut butter, while her faithful hound licked it off with enthusiasm.

Dunbar Innocence

In the seaside resort of Dunbar, the first time that one is with another person is still held to be special, in a way that has been lost in larger metropolises. A young woman, barely past her eighteenth birthday, had still not favoured any of the numerous advances she had received, so intent was she on finding both the right man and time.

On one of her frequent nights out in Edinburgh, it appeared that the moment had arrived. She and her friends had been enjoying a fun evening at one of the many top-notch establishments that pepper Lothian Road. At a particularly happening karaoke bar, the group met with another group, composed entirely of men. While most of the men were boisterous, one alone appeared shy and reclusive, despite being easily the most handsome of the bunch. Coaxing him into conversation, it soon became apparent to the girl from Dunbar that he and she shared many interests. While their companions lurched from one obscene joke to another, this couple formed an alliance of the purest infatuation.

When the time came for the last bus home, they could not be separated. One of her friends, sensing the occasion, offered them the use of her mattress. The next morning the young woman awoke feeling the wonder of life pulsing through her Dunbar body. Turning over to embrace her tender bedmate, she discovered him gone.

Looking around the room, there was no trace of his clothes. Having no way to contact him, and knowing he did not have her number, the next few days were spent in misery, until she was, eventually, able to appreciate those brief few hours for what they had been.

Some two weeks had passed when, sitting at her work station performing a mail-merge operation on her computer, the young woman felt a slight stirring inside her. By lunchtime this had developed into a painful internal itch. By half-past five the affliction had intensified to the point where she felt no option but to go directly to the accident and emergency unit of the nearest hospital.

Crippled with discomfort, she stumbled out of the taxi and into the waiting-room where vigilant staff assigned her swiftly to a nearby bed. With breathtaking efficiency a doctor arrive, performed a thorough examination and was able to administer both pain-killing and antibiotic treatments, as well as a number of tests.

The young lady was kept in overnight, her parents arriving the next morning to be by her side. Around noon the same doctor came to her bedside to ask a number of routine questions. After listening to the girl's answers, he explained that the results of some tests he had asked for the previous evening had come back.

'There is little to worry about,' he explained, 'although you do have a serious infection of a sexual nature.'

The girl blushed and her parents frowned.

'A short course of penicillin-based drugs will be sufficient to cure you, but I must ask for the identity of all of your recent sexual partners.'

'Why is that?' enquired the girl.

'Because this type of infection can only be caught from having sexual intercourse with a corpse.'

Shocked, the girl burst into tears.

The man with whom she had enjoyed the single night of passion in her young life was finally traced, with the help of the bar staff in the pub where the two had met. He, in turn, was eventually sacked from his position as an assistant in the local mortuary.

The young lady was never allowed to return to the family home.

Fat Deterrence

Scots truck drivers are not generally small. Yet few know the reasons for their specially trained physical frames.

Some time ago a Scottish articulated lorry driver from Cupar was driving through South England when he spotted a man standing by the side of the road next to a car parked with its bonnet up. Thinking the man was in trouble, and being every inch the kind person that his mother had brought him up to be, the lorry driver pulled his rig over and went to get out of his cabin.

But as he opened the door, he found the same man now standing below him, pointing what appeared to be a gun in his direction. Angrily, the man demanded that the truck driver get out.

Changing from 'kind' to 'protective', the lorry driver remembered his cargo of tinned produce from one of Scotland's finest food companies. No wonder he was being targeted for theft. Dutifully, he shook his head and refused to climb down. At this, the man reached up and yanked at the truck driver's arm, still resting on the cabin door. Pulled from below, the bulky Scotsman tumbled out of the cabin, landing on top of his assailant, and breaking a few of the robber's limbs in the process. The police took care of the rest.

As word of this event spread among Scottish truck drivers via CB radio and service-station chatter, the moral of the story was not lost. Ever since then Scottish truck drivers have been fighting a battle to ensure that their weight is consistently high enough to crush any would-be highwaymen.

Mystery Hawick Assassin

It was a particularly hot day in Hawick when an elderly woman pulled into the car park of a well-known local supermarket. Taking off her jacket and leaving it on the back seat of the car, she noticed that there was a man in the neighbouring vehicle who seemed to be asleep on the steering-wheel, his left hand resting on the back of his head. Thinking this a bit strange, but presuming that he was simply a husband waiting for his wife to come back with the shopping, the elderly woman continued with her business. Yet when she returned some half hour later, having been held up at the reduced-price counter, the lady felt that the continued presence of the man on his steering-wheel required further investigation. Tapping solicitously on the window, she noticed that the man was not asleep.

'Help,' he gasped through pursed lips. 'Please call 999. I've been shot in the back of the head and I can feel my brains coming out!'

The elderly woman then saw that there did indeed appear to be a sticky matter oozing between the fingers of the man's hand. Alarmed, she dashed back into the supermarket and called for an ambulance and the police.

With the car surrounded by armed officers and the rest of the shopping area evacuated, a paramedic opened the car door and then inspected the man's wound. After some prodding and sniffing, the medic then raised something to his lips, before looking down into the back seat of the car. Then he burst out laughing and signaled for the all clear.

It transpired that the man in the car had been sitting in his car when a pack of pre-prepared croissant mix had exploded, launching both the metal lid and a volley of dough into the back of his head. Slightly concussed by this, the unfortunate gentleman had then feared the worst when feeling the dough mix sticking to his hair. As a mark of sympathy for man and the ordeal he had endured in their car park, the supermarket were pleased to present him with a replacement tin of croissant mix, and a bottle of shampoo.

Kirkcaldy Turkey

The need for a good turkey at Christmas is an innate part of the Kirkcaldy soul. The idea that the special day might arrive and that the family table would be without the traditional bird, is not acceptable. Thus, despite the economic circumstances, people will do what they have to do to maintain the delicate Yuletide balance.

Staff at a bright new supermarket in the Fife town were incredibly busy. With just one week to go, the shop was full with festive-season shoppers, although the presence of a festive atmosphere was limited to the party hats being worn by the two girls at the cheese counter.

An elderly woman, sternly wrapped in snorkel parka and knee-length winter skirt, was making her way forward as part of the nine-items-or-less queue. Perhaps because of the pressing of those around, she appeared most weary, her eyes fluttering in the artificial luminescence. As she reached the till her entire body flopped against it, and the seasonal worker manning the conveyor belt pressed a special button to call for help.

Within seconds a smartly jacketed assistant manager was there, guiding the old woman towards a convenient seat. Such is the concern of the supermarket staff for those who provide their custom.

As the woman seemed to waver in and out of consciousness, she gave an abrupt yelp and from the bottom of the snorkel jacket a large frozen turkey escaped, thumping the floor. As tears of impoverished humiliation streamed down the old lady's face, the assistant manager, regretfully, called the police.

The woman got a suspended sentence. The turkey got put back.

Relaxed Welcome

Although all pubs in Fraserburgh are famous for the couthy, charming welcome they provide to guests, one in particular was known for its hospitality. This *bon hommie* revolved around the happy figure of the proprietor, a large local man who would sit in his chair near the bar, conversing with anyone and everyone who entered while his dutiful wife kept order behind the bar.

On a dreech November day the host did not seem to be his usual welcoming self. No amount of jovial probing could produce any form of pithy response. Furthermore the landlady herself seemed far from at ease.

At length one of the locals called another local, who was a doctor. The doctor arrived and within moments had pronounced the man dead. Later, under police investigation, it turned out that the publican had died the night before whilst having a bath. Fearful of the impact of this on the business, his wife had tried to pretend that all was well.

Informed of the lack of provision for her future welfare, and the huge gambling debts the husband had secretly run up, the court did not punish the woman too much, even though the penalty for the ancient Scots crime of 'keeping a dead body' is severe. The pub remains open, although the chat is now not so good.

Ding

On a rainy day, a tearful old woman appeared in a pawnshop off the Royal Mile in central Edinburgh, with a brand new microwave strapped to the top of her battered tartan shopping-trolley. Lugging the electric machine on to the top of the counter, she asked how much it might be worth. The slightly taken aback assistant considered the new-looking device and asked if it was still working.

'Aye,' the old lady, uttered through dry, weary lips, 'but it has brought me sorrow.'

Lifting the otherwise shiny contraption closer to him, the shop assistant noticed a faint spot of red liquid apparently leaking from the door. At the same time he became aware of a distasteful reek, of something fetid and unholy in the air around him. Staring through the smoked glass of the microwave door, he struggled to understand the uneven coating on the white walls within. Lifting his head, he stared blankly at his elderly customer.

'My son bought me this last week.'

The pawn man then listened as the woman told of how it was her custom to dry her pet dog Muffy off in her old gas oven when they came home after a traditional wet walk in The Meadows area of the city.

'About gas mark 1, with the door slightly open. Three minutes usually does it.'

Sniffling, she explained how, having heard the wonders of the microwave, she had placed the little terrier in for 'just a wee burst'.

'He'd only been in for a few seconds when there was a terrible yowling.'

At this the old lady could continue no longer and, after a consoling cup of tea in the manager's office, she was offered a complimentary taxi ride home. The staff drew lots to decide who would scrape out and cleanse the microwave, which was eventually sold for a remarkably good price to a nice student unaware of its cruel heritage.

Prêt à Morte

Oban has many distinguished retailers but one of them stands out as the place to shop for female clothing. Well-recognised throughout the Highlands, the store operates a generous, almost lenient, returns policy, allowing the well-heeled ladies of those parts to take goods home and receive appropriate advice from their fashion-oriented families, many of whom are known to use the Internet to keep abreast of trends in Milan, Paris and Inverness. Yet in flagrant violation of the spirit of the store's 'try after you buy' stance, it was not unknown for some women to buy expensive outfits, wear them out to church or a local ball, and then return them to the store for a full refund, having skimmed the clothes through a local dry cleaner on the way back.

While aware of this behaviour, the store chose to ignore it rather than run the risk of offending good customers. Yet one occurrence forced them to reconsider. A woman had bought a splendid dress, only to return it two days later complaining of a skin condition, and attaching a bill from her fancy dermatologist. The note explained the presence in the woman's epidermis of formaldehyde.

Eager to track down the cause, an investigation into the splendid dress was launched forthwith. A check through the firm's receipts brought out an awkward explanation. The garment had previously been purchased by another

woman who, when confronted with the evidence, explained that she had bought the dress, not for herself but
for her recently deceased sister, that she might be nicely
attired for her funeral service. Following the ceremony,
the woman – keen not to lose her monies – had secured
the dress from the undertakers, before returning it to the
store.

Preferring silence, the store kept this aspect of the tale
quiet, paying the second customer's medical bill and
recouping, in part, their losses through the third sale
of the properly cleaned item some two weeks later.

Dundee Naughtiness

Dundee is famous for the affection that its citizens extend to all things natural. No dog, cat or tortoise goes without a home for long in the self-styled City of Discovery.

One husband in the East Coast town was particularly devoted to caring for his pedigree beagle, Whittaker. Every evening, as soon as dinner was finished, gentle Whittaker was taken for a long walk. The man's wife was quite happy with this arrangement. It allowed her husband to relax from his stressful banking job, whilst also getting him and Whittaker out from under her feet for a good part of the night. Both were always most content on their return.

There came one evening when the husband had not arrived home by the usual time. His wife was not unduly concerned. Sure enough, a few minutes later there was a telephone call from her husband, explaining that there had been a breakdown in one of the bank's IT systems and that he had to stay late to oversee the necessary repairs. The husband then asked that his wife take Whittaker the beagle out for his usual evening walk.

Pleased to oblige on this one occasion, the nice wife put Whittaker on his lead and wandered out the front door, unsure which route to take. As it transpired, she need not have worried. Whittaker knew where he wanted to go. Within moments the wife found herself being dragged along the street by the purposeful beagle, intent on some destination of which she was unaware.

In due course they arrived at an anonymous street some 15 minutes' hard walk from their own home. Somewhat puzzled by this course, the wife was suddenly on the move once more as Whittaker yanked her towards the front door of a semi-detached house. Arriving at the door the dog began jumping up and scratching at the glass panels, despite the attempted restraint of his owner. Then an attractive young woman, dressed only in a skimpy dressing-gown, pulled the door open. Without hesitation Whittaker bolted into the house, pursued by both women.

The wife stumbled into the living-room to find her dog jumping on to the sofa, where lay the prostrate semi-naked figure of her husband.

Cashmere Ending

The New Town of Edinburgh is home to many cat lovers. A wealthy lady, who lived on her own in a magnificent town house, was nevertheless aware that with Cashmere, her Burmese cat, getting on in years, it might be a good idea to move to more peaceful surroundings, so that the loyal feline might enjoy his last few years in a calm and peaceful environment, away from the fast cars and careless feet that are so often the undoing of the elderly, less-responsive cat.

Settling on a country house near Dalwhinney, the move was arranged with all the smooth speed that inherited money can buy. Within a few weeks Cashmere and his owner were stepping over the doorstep of their new home.

They had only just arrived, and the French windows of the dining-room had barely been opened for a view of the Highland vista, when Cashmere began calling for his dinner. Pleased that he had settled in so quickly, his owner trotted off to the kitchen to cut up some of the steak that Cashmere preferred. Arriving back with his special plate, Cashmere's well-to-do owner was just in time to see her faithful companion being carried off in the talons of a golden eagle.

Peebles Mastermind

A Scottish student in Birmingham was enjoying herself too much. The nights were endless socialising and the days were spent in contemplation of fashion articles. At weekends the two activities merged in a morass of big city hedonism. As the end of term approached, the young woman realised that she needed to correct the trajectory of her course. Going back to Peebles with a 'Fail' after her name would not be acceptable, not in a town where academic qualifications are very much the standard by which all offspring are measured.

Sensing a chance at the first big exam of the year, the young lady picked up two examination books when she entered the hall. One she left blank, slipping it into her mini backpack when no one was looking. The other she pretended to write in throughout the examination period.

As the clock struck twelve and the examiner told all to stop writing, the teenager scribbled a note on the first page.

'Dear Mum and Dad. I have just finished my Chemistry exam and wanted to tell you both how much I love you and appreciate all the sacrifices you have made to get me here.' She then handed this paper in.

Rushing home, the girl then completed the exam questions at her own desk, making full use of all of her reference books, before rushing to catch the next postal collection. Later that day she was able to act completely surprised when she received a telephone call from the university, explaining that 'there had been some kind of mix-up'. Listening aghast to what had happened, the student then received permission to have her mother send the correct paper to the Head of Department by return post. This her mother duly did, ensuring her daughter enjoyed both a good mark, and a good time that night.

Luxury Scone

A couple from Aberdeen had occasion to visit Edinburgh and, finding themselves near one of its most celebrated department stores, sought refuge from the shopping masses in the esteemed establishments's tasty coffee shop. Something of particular interest on the exquisitely laminated menu was the store's own-brand 'luxury scone'. Never having had a 'luxury scone', the couple from Aberdeen could not restrain themselves, opting to half one between them. So magnificent was the taste that they felt that life up North would be much improved by an on-going presence of the scone in their lives. Thus determined, they called over the young waitress.

'That was brilliant. Could we get a copy of the recipe?' they asked.

'I'm afraid not,' replied the waitress.

The couple conferred briefly, before asking, 'Would it be possible to buy a copy of the recipe?'

A posh smile crossed the waitress' face.

'Yes,' she said.

'How much?'

'Just three fifty,' she replied.

The couple asked for the amount to be added to their bill and, settling by credit card, departed, the recipe nestling inside a splendidly branded paper bag, with real string handles.

One month and many scones later, the husband received his Visa statement, at the bottom of which was the line, 'Luxury scone recipe: £350.00'.

'That's outrageous!' he declared, and telephoned the department store. The store refused to move.

'Our waitress quoted you a fair price for the recipe of the luxury scone. You should have queried this at the time of purchase.' Like so many, the couple reflected on how they had simply signed without checking.

Undaunted, they continued to call the store in far-away Edinburgh, demanding that the management see sense.

'Under no circumstances will this money be refunded. We now consider the matter closed,' was the final line in the final letter the couple received. Two weeks later the wife had an injunction taken out against her, barring her from making any more phone calls or sending any further letters to the store's general manager.

At this point the husband contacted the store with an offer. If they would refund the money, he would forget the whole thing. Otherwise, he would personally ensure that the luxury scone recipe was distributed as widely as possible, free of charge. Shortly before he was arrested for blackmail, he managed to send off twenty copies of the recipe to close friends, urging them to pass it on to twenty more each. Additionally, he posted it on several websites, some of which have now been closed down. This is the recipe:

Luxury Scones
Makes approximately ten
8 oz expensive self-raising flour
1/2 teaspoon good salt
2 oz best margarine
1 oz finest white sugar
2 oz select sultanas and currants
1 free-range organic egg, beaten with sufficient full-cream milk to make 1/4 pint of liquid

Mix flour and salt with care. Rub in margarine thoroughly, using all digits (wash hands most carefully). Stir in sugar and fruit. Add egg and milk mixture, reserving a bit for brushing over tops later. Knead lightly on a floured surface and then roll out to just over inch thickness. Cut into 2-inch rounds. Get friend or neighbour to confirm all measurements are correct. Re-roll trimmings and cut more rounds.

Place rounds on a greased baking tray and then brush the tops with egg and milk using a fine camel-hair brush. Bake in an oven at 220°C (425°F or gas mark 7), for ten minutes, or until they look nice and are simultaneously soft and spongy. Handle lightly for best results.

Bird Bullet

The journey from Edinburgh to Inverness by train is not famed for its speed. Towards achieving a much faster journey time, Scotrail are developing a high-speed loco-motive capable of beating the French TGV and thus reducing the journey North to a mere hour or so. Such an accomplishment needs to be done with total safety in mind. To this end, the engineers needed to ensure that the windshield of the new train could withstand the high pressures sustained at top speed, and any encounters with the low-flying game birds of Scotland. One engineer had heard of a machine developed by the Federal Aviation Authority in the United States. This gun-type device is used to similar effect to test the strength of windshields on airplanes. A dead chicken is fired at the glass at about the speed that the aircraft usually travels. If the windshield does not break, then it is likely to survive a real collision.

Suitably impressed, the design team in Scotland or-dered one of the machines. Setting it up with meticulous care in their development facility outside Methil, they fired a dead chicken at the approximate speed of the train. To their astonishment and against all predictions the bird went through the windshield, breaking the top off the driver's seat and making a large dent in the rear wall of the cabin. Repeating the experiment only resulted in similar damage. Alarmed, they paid for an FAA engineer to be flown over from the United States to check their testing procedure. On arrival, the engineer inspected all test components, before recommending that they try again, but this time without using a chicken that was frozen.

Good Companion

Not too far from the spirited bustle of Aviemore is a country house of some distinction. The young lady of the house, a future student of faraway London, was left alone for the evening whilst her parents enjoyed a Rotary Club function. Pleased of the opportunity to pass a quiet night before the television in the company of Kipper, the family's friendly cocker spaniel, the soon-to-be student set herself up with popcorn, crisps and a glass of the family wine. While watching the news, she was alarmed to hear that the police had advised of the escape from an institution of a dangerous deviant, who should not be approached under any circumstances. Fortifying herself with more wine, the young woman toured the house, faithful Kipper by her side, checking all the windows and doors. Satisfied of her safety, she watched the start of a bad late movie before retiring to bed with a book, diligent Kipper nestling beneath the old brass bedstead. As the wind blew outside, the dog would occasionally whimper or growl, causing the teenager to lower her hand over the bed for the friendly dog to lick, in an act of canine self-mollification.

Soon enough, the young woman found herself falling asleep and, resting the hardback novel on the ground, she simultaneously switched out the light whilst administering a 'goodnight' stroke to Kipper.

Not one hour later she awoke with a start. Sitting bolt upright, the girl struggled to assure herself that she had not heard the sound of a window being opened. Looking over she could see it was shut. Besides, all of the windows in the house had been checked. Resting her hand over the side of the bed, Kipper's re-assuring lick told her all was well. Sleep pulled her under.

Yet not too much later this sleep was again broken as the young woman woke abruptly. Convinced that she had heard something, she got out of bed, went on to the landing and looked over the heavy wooden banister. There was nothing. Ambling back to bed, the woman heard the faintest of noises but, unable to identify it clearly, she put it down to the wind and pulled the covers over her once more. Yet dangling her hand over the side, and feeling the friendly lick once more, the girl became convinced that she could hear a drip, drip, drip coming from the bathroom. Throwing the duvet back, she ran, angry with herself, through to the adjoining room. Flicking the light switch, the bright fluorescence rendered her temporarily blind. But as the flickering ceased, she was able to make out a shape dangling from the shower head. Peering closely, clad only in her fun pyjamas, the girl realised it was the mutilated body of Kipper, his throat slashed allowing a steady trickle of blood on to the tiled floor. Turning, her eyes caught the words, written in red on the bathroom mirror, 'Humans can lick too.'

Stranraer Banns

There was a most lavish wedding reception in Stranraer, the type for which the coastal town has long been famed in Western matrimonial business circles. The bridesmaids were resplendent in shiny red, flanking the two-tone silk bride in a tribute of enduring memory. All of the menfolk had an aspect of tartan, and even the minister was defiantly tailored in lustrous black of the finest cloth.

Arriving at the professionally-erected marquee – so smoothly tacked on to the back door of the hotel – the guests crammed buoyantly in to await the feast of many courses, with whisky at the end. Following the delicious main course, plates of extravagant size were brought in, each bearing upon it a nest of chocolate dobs filled with cream, which one or two present knew to be no less than profiteroles. Falling upon these with feverish delight, the guests had soon cleared their way through to the gleaming ceramic, whereupon they sat back to await more drink and the traditional speeches.

No sooner had the best man stood up to the sing-song cheering of all present, than he found himself interrupted – by none other than the bridegroom himself. Presuming this to be the preamble to some offer of further free spirits, the crowd quietened itself solemnly while the bridegroom gathered himself. Then he spoke.

'Many thanks to all of you for being here today. My

thanks also for the gifts you have so kindly delivered, offered or promised. At this stage I must thank my in-laws for their wonderful donation of two prime weeks of timeshare in Portugal for our honeymoon. I am sure my wife will enjoy her time there. I will not, because I am not going.'

At this the humour of the moment vanished, as the gathering recognised a change in atmosphere not familiar to such occasions. The bridegroom continued.

'I am not going to Portugal. I am going to the Bahamas. When I return, I will be seeking an annulment of our marriage, with immediate effect. Nor do I intend to 'chip in' for half of the cost of this day, as I had suggested that I might. I appreciate that this might be a shock for some of you, but if you would all now take a look at the bottom of your plates, everything will become much clearer.'

As one, the marquee raised their plates of extravagant size, turning them over to reveal a photograph of the bride and best man in a position of intense fleshy communion. After waiting for all present to consume the image, the bridegroom turned to his best man and wished him well in life, before offering the same blessing to his wife. He then left, never to return to the seaside town.

Most people went home after that.

Well Done

Countryside exploration is a favoured pursuit for many of the small children of Stirling. The local fields and farms are home to many nooks and crannies where youngsters can hide and play. Small woods and the like can yield unexpected treasure.

One afternoon, two small boys were running around in farmland near Bridge of Allan. Stumbling through bushes, they found a hole in the ground, perfectly circular, with brick walls and no apparent bottom. Seeking information on its depth, the two boys dropped a stone down the hole and listened. After a long time there was a faint splash. Looking around, the boys found a larger stone and dropped that down too. Then an even larger stone, and soon they were throwing everything they could find down the abandoned well, with the type of mindless gusto only small boys can muster.

As their store of ammunition began to run down, they cast their net in a wider circle.

'Hey, look at this!' one of them cried. It was a large, heavy metal spike, dug firmly into the earth.

Getting on their knees, the two boys set about digging the spike out. Then, together, they carried it to the hole and hurled it in with glee.

It was only when the spike was in mid-air that they noticed a chain attached to it that had been dragging behind them in the undergrowth. As they watched both chain and spike fall and disappear into the darkness, they heard a noise behind them. Turning, they saw the shape of a large Alsatian dog, tied to the chain, being pulled through the bushes. Before they knew what to do, the yelping dog was whizzing past them and down to a watery end.

Baggage Handlers

A couple from Linlithgow were on holiday in Ayrshire. Their rural cottage was a most modern and fanciful affair. There was all manner of hi-tech kitchen equipment, from a cordless kettle to an electric tin-opener. The television was wide and the curtains swished along their rail with unparalleled ease. Each bedroom had a box of tissues in a floral cotton container.

Spending most of their time walking on the beach and sitting in the garden, the couple were most at ease. One night, though, they decided to walk to the nearest village, a journey of two miles or so, in order to enjoy a night of beer and local atmosphere.

Arriving in the bar, they soon settled in, and it wasn't long before they were drawn into conversation with several of the village folk.

'And where are you staying?' somebody enquired.

The couple explained and everyone went a bit quiet. Sensing the change in ambience, the husband asked what was amiss. After a bit of hush-hushing, an older woman who'd had a few pints already explained that, 'although it's just rumour, mind you', there were those who thought that the Scots–Italian owners of the cottage had links to the Mafia. At this point all those listening laughed, but there could be no doubting the sincerity of the nervous air that hung between them. The conversation moved on.

Returning to their lovely cottage later that night, the Linlithgow couple were alarmed to find the front door swinging wide open. Dashing inside, the husband soon came back to report that they had been burgled. All of their suitcases were gone, along with sundry personal items.

Going inside, they remembered the note that had been left for them, 'in case of emergency', with the telephone number of the cottage owners at the bottom. Feeling at a loss, they telephoned this number and explained what had happened. The voice at the end of the line was friendly and reassuring. Don't call the police tonight, they said. It's a long way to the nearest station and it won't make any difference. Just go to bed and try and get some sleep.

Awaking the next morning with every intention of calling the police, the wife came downstairs and was leafing through the directory when she heard a knock at the door, then the sound of a car speeding off. Opening the door, she found all of their stolen possessions sitting on the doorstep.

Kilmarnock Symbolic Gesture

Things oriental are popular with the younger inhabitants of Kilmarnock, allowing them to express themselves in ways that demonstrate a sensitivity to world culture. A local lass, keen to keep up with the latest trend, wished to get a tattoo on her left shoulder, picked out in Chinese characters.

The family being without a Chinese dictionary, the young lady asked one of her father's friends who was going to Hong Kong on business to bring back some language materials for her consideration. One week later these items appeared, a huge assortment of menus, brochures and tourist material. From these the girl picked out a particularly striking series of characters, took the train into Glasgow and had the set pierced into her skin in an intense afternoon session.

That weekend her friends were suitably impressed as they wandered to and fro among the high spots of the Kilmarnock nightlife. More amused than impressed were the Cantonese owners of a local Chinese takeaway, who watched a bare-shouldered teenager walking past with the phrase 'This dish cheap but very tasty' displayed on her back.

Auld Grey Toon Kwik-Fix

English students at the University of St Andrews are renowned for their wily ways, resorting to all manner of activities to avoid studying, and always with an eye open for the chance to get good marks without strenuous effort. Radio transmitters, small mirrors and tiny notebooks have all been confiscated during exams.

One year two particularly self-confident individuals from the home counties were determined to have a good time on the night before one of their important History exams. Partying late into the night at a country residence, they woke well after the test had started. Driving into town at a pace of more leisure than urgency, they arrived as everyone else was leaving the exam hall. Presenting themselves before the stern Scottish Professor of History, they explained how, on the way in that morning, their car had experienced a puncture and that, despite their best efforts to contact the breakdown services, they had been unavoidably delayed. Would it be possible for them to take the exam now?

The Scot considered their request, then smiled. Of course that would be possible. But why rush it? After their stressful morning, would it not be better to take the test next week, once they had recovered themselves. Overjoyed at this unexpected generosity of spirit, the two students spent most of the weekend talking with friends about the likely contents of the exam, and the rest of the time in the pub, pugnaciously confident.

Arriving at the department on the Monday morning, the students were shown into separate rooms, where one member of staff was waiting to supervise them. It was explained to each that the exam would have two sections. They were then given the exam papers.

The first section, worth 15 per cent of the total mark, was a simple multiple-choice selection of questions on historical events. The second section, worth 85 per cent of the total mark, consisted of one question only: 'Which tyre on your car was punctured?'

The two students did eventually graduate, from a nice modern college in a small town somewhere near Norwich.

A Day Wasted

Travel is not familiar to the natives of Hawick. They regard each day out of the Borders town as 'a day wasted'. Still, for the sake of the local industry they are willing to forsake their home. Thus, a young married man set off for the Far East in search of sales for the famous knitwear company of which he and the rest of the town are so proud. Naturally, this being his first trip abroad, his family were full of advice, notably his mother who advised him 'not to speak with anybody who is overly friendly' – advice the man had received from childhood concerning visits to Edinburgh and Galashiels.

Having carried his large case of sample garments from Asian city to Asian city, the young man was nearing his final stop, Bangkok. With successful visits to Hong Kong, Tokyo and Seoul behind him, he approached this last city with a sense of confidence and triumph. Sure enough, within a couple of days he had secured more purchase orders than any of his firm's previous visitors. Faxing the details back to head office, he felt the sort of proud vigour that only success on behalf of a small Scottish business can bring.

With the end of his travel approaching, he decided to relax a little. Until this point he had stayed in his hotel room each night, alone and focused, gearing himself up for each presentation. Sitting in the plush hotel bar, he now found himself composed in the exciting alien environment. After a beer or two, he was even more composed. While sitting, minding his own affairs, thinking of his far-away wife and children, he did not notice the young Thai lady moving seat by seat towards him over the course of an hour. As midnight grew closer, so did she and soon the young Hawick man found himself in conversation with this beautiful woman, whose English was most refined. At one point, he felt her hand on his lap.

The next thing that the man from Hawick remembered was waking up in his bath tub. His head felt terrible, far worse than the result of a few beers. It took a few seconds before he realised that bath was filled with ice-cubes, and that he was somehow restricted in movement. Pinned to the wall next to his head was a note, 'DO NOT MOVE! CALL THE EMERGENCY OPERATOR'.

Panic-stricken, the man reached over and lifted the receiver on the wall of the hotel bathroom. As he explained his situation, the operator interrupted.

'Please reach behind you,' she said. 'Is there a tube sticking out of your lower back?'

The man moved his hand round behind him and felt the protruding tube. As he started to cry with fear, the operator was already calling for an ambulance. She was familiar with the practice of drugging Western business travellers and removing their kidneys for sale.

SCOTTISH URBAN MYTHS

The last conscious thoughts of the young man, only midway through his twenties, were for his wife and children back in the green valleys of the Scottish Borders.

Tarbert Pet Rescue

A weekend escape from the exhilarating grind of the 24-hour, non-stop Glasgow life is the goal of many of its urban professionals. Getting into the country allows them not only to wind down after days on end spent in meetings, traffic jams and not-quite-there designer suits, but also to pretend that there was a good reason for buying an enormous four-wheel drive vehicle.

One such couple prided themselves on being real fans of the natural world. When not leafing through wine club brochures, they liked nothing more than watching well-made television documentaries and programmes where domestic pets did cute things. Taking a croft just outside Tarbert one weekend, they arrived early, eager to get off and into the woods. Within minutes of parking their cheap Land Rover imitation car, they were striding through the trees, relishing every breath of the so-fresh air.

Coming back they heard a noise near their feet. Looking down, the woman announced, 'It's a puppy!' The man looked to where she was pointing. Sure enough, there on the ground, trembling and frightened, was a small brown puppy, its eyes watching them with appre-hension.

Recognising its fear, the woman bent down and hushed it, taking a piece of energy bar from her pocket and placing it before the timid dog. Ravenous, it wolfed the tit-bit down. From then it was only a matter of minutes before she was able to coax the nervous animal into her arms, where it nestled, still trembling, on the walk back to the cottage.

It was too late to go into Tarbert by the time they got back, so instead they washed the animal in the bath before giving it some more food and milk. Going to bed, both of them were concerned about its welfare – the puppy had not stopped trembling – and both agreed that it would be best for it to sleep, safe and warm, at the end of their bed.

The shock of being bitten in the middle of the night was enough to make the man scream out loud. Jumping up, the city couple caught site of the timid pup rushing through the bedroom door and downstairs.

It took two hours to lure the poor wee thing out from behind the cooker, during which time a vet was called to see what ailed the creature so. Meanwhile, the man applied some antiseptic cream to his big toe.

On arrival, the vet opened the cardboard box in which the pup was huddled, took one look, closed it, picked the box up and started to walk out.

'That's not a pup – it's a pregnant sewer rat. Something has bitten its tail off, which is why you didn't realise it was a rat. That's also why it's trembling. Probably still in a state of shock. You'd better get to the doctor.'

Later, lying in the hospital, having already had tetanus and several other jabs and awaiting the intensely painful stomach injections that are required to treat potential rabies victims, the much-pained man was able to consider with his woman the virtues of city life.

Portobello Harvest

Portobello is a wonderful seaside village near Edinburgh, which still preserves many of the polite customs long lost to its big, worldly neighbour. It was not so many decades ago that something strange was found on the lovely beach that is so important to the gentle settlement's identity and economy.

Strolling with her dog in the dawn light, a librarian was amazed to find the massive body of a whale sitting in the low surf. A hastily arranged visit from the local vet confirmed that the animal was dead.

As news of this discovery spread around town, the beach filled with sightseers. Soon there was a circus of stalls selling traditional baked food stuffs and souvenir T-shirts. People jostled to have their photographs taken standing next to the sad beast.

After a few days, during which they were happy to reap the economic harvest from the unexpected cetaceous guest, the Portobello authorities began to address the issue of what to do next with the corpse. Local butchers advised that the meat would soon begin to rot and that the smell from such a huge animal would be great and long-lasting. The profitable business of weekend beach visits might be threatened.

Fearing that the tide of fortune might yet turn against them, the authorities decided to act swiftly and decisively.

The received advice was that merely burying the whale would be insufficient, as the daily tides would soon wash away the covering sand. No, the powers that be decided that it would be best to dynamite the animal to oblivion.

Explosives experts arrived and set about placing their charges around and inside the body. After a day, they were ready.

The entire population gathered at the top of the beach, held back by safety ropes. On a count of three, the button was pushed and an almighty explosion filled the air. As the smoke cleared, it became apparent that the whale had vanished. Then, from above, the people and streets of Portobello were assailed by the millions of tiny pieces of whale blubber landing all around. Some large pieces knocked one or two children down, and there were many screams and cries of terror.

The experts had miscalculated how much dynamite to use. Rather than breaking the body up, they had obliterated it. It was seven days before the streets of Portobello were offal-free, and during this time many cats grew in size enormously. To this day locals often refer to so-called experts as 'blubberheads'.

Inside Story

It had been several years since anyone had visited the elderly aunt, long consigned to one of the Dundee's most celebrated institutions. One Christmas, the youngest niece took it upon herself to give her old relative a Yuletide treat. Setting off for the hospital in bitterly cold weather, the young woman wrapped herself up with care, arriving at the tall, iron gates tired but warm.

Although there were several patients wandering around the lobby and entrance hall, there was no sign of the staff. Venturing into one of the wards, the woman was greeted by a nurse, who asked who she was looking for. The woman explained and the nurse's expression changed dramatically. Escorting the visitor to a nearby empty social room, the nurse explained that, regretfully, the elderly aunt had died one month previously, and that the hospital had not known whom to contact. Sensing the woman's distress, the nurse said that she would get one of the senior consultants, who would be able to provide fuller details, and noted that she would also arrange for a cup of tea. Finally, recognising that the young woman was over-wrapped for the well-heated old building, the nurse offered to hang up her warm coat and gloves.

Still shocked by the news, it was some time before the young woman realised that neither doctor nor tea had arrived. Going out into the corridor, she was immediately seized by two white-coated large men, who forced her into a straitjacket and then into a secure cell. The young woman struggled fiercely, announcing, 'I'm not mad – I work in Tesco.'

'That's what they all say,' the orderlies replied, before locking the door.

The woman's keys, cards and relevant ID had been in her coat. Her protestations of sanity simply confirmed what everyone knew – she was insane. It was five long years before she was able to obtain release. The patient who had posed as the helpful nurse was never found.

Sticky Decision

The case of the Kirkcaldy jelly continues to rumble through the courts. A woman, fully funded by Legal Aid, is suing a well-known high-street chain of chemists that sold her a tub of contraceptive jelly.

Rather than applying the material as intended, the woman ate the jelly, having spread it on some toast and becoming pregnant.

'If you're not meant to eat it then it shouldn't be called jelly. Jelly is for putting in your mouth. Well, it is where I come from.'

Lawyers for the woman have successfully argued that placing the product only three aisles from the sandwich and soft drink section was deliberately misleading.

'When one is in a state of sexual arousal, it is unreasonable to expect someone to read beyond the labelling of an item. Under the circumstances, our client has been dreadfully misled.'

A claim for several hundred thousand pounds is now destined for settlement in the European Court of Justice, where professional views are divided. The shop assistant who sold the woman the product is herself off work as a result of stress from the case. Her manager is scathing.

'That woman is well known to be on the fiddle with every claim that can be had. Our town might the home of Adam Smith, but this is taking private enterprise too far.'

A spokesman for the manufacturers of the contraceptive jelly is equally unimpressed.

'Quite frankly this sort of thing is coming up more and more. We're shortly going to be changing the description of toothpaste, as people are already suing us in Belgium and Italy because they can't stick things together with it.'

Well-placed solicitors believe the Kirkcaldy woman has an excellent chance of winning.

Fort William Outdoor Leisure

The barbecue season in Fort William is short but joyous. There is much competition between rival families as to who can produce the best ribs and so forth, and passed-down recipes for garnish are fiercely guarded.

One couple were renowned for their hospitality and their events were much appreciated and attended. This particular year was no exception. As was customary, everyone had arrived well before the food was due and large quantities of own-brand home wine had turned the back garden into a place of festive summer fun. The hosts for the day were happy to join in with the merrymaking, and soon both were at one with the spirit of their guests.

The throwing of pieces of food forms part of the celebratory nature of these occasions. and so it was that one particular sausage of the underdone variety found itself being hurled skyward, coming to rest midway down the uncompleted patio. Here the sausage sat, until the man of the house, on his way back from relief in the bushes, stepped on it, up-ending himself and fracturing his ankle in the process.

While many occasions might have ground to a halt at such a break, this was a gathering of stronger constitution. So while the husband was taken to the nearest hospital in a taxi, his guests continued to mingle uproariously.

Returning in due course, the husband found his family

clearing up the remnants of a thoroughly good time. He sat down with his new plastercast in the front-room, weary of body and mind, and took comfort from a well-deserved cigarette. Outside his wife, finding what was left of the paraffin which they had used to ignite the barbecue, emptied the contents of the can into the bushes at the bottom of the garden, before settling down to do the dishes. A few minutes later the husband, needing to use the bathroom but being unable to ascend the stairs with comfort, hobbled out to the same bushes he had used previously, dropped his trousers and then, on dropping his still lit cigarette into the paraffin-soaked undergrowth, facilitated a second visit to the hospital, for third-degree burns of a particularly painful nature.

Leave a Message

Accommodation can be hard to come by for Edinburgh students. Over the busy tourist seasons, landlords take back their flats for more lucrative deals. So sometimes friends have to 'double up' for these periods.

One Hogmanay, Sandra and Margaret were sharing a room in an area of the city popular with undergraduates. Around 9 p.m. one evening, Sandra remembered that her library book was due back that day and that the library closed at 11 p.m. She told Margaret that she was going to the library to return the book and would probably go for a drink after. Sandra invited her to come along, but Margaret declined, having an early start the next day at the train station coffee shop where she worked part-time. Margaret asked Sandra to put the lights out as she left. Sandra did so and headed for the library, enjoying the chill night air as she crossed the frost-struck Meadows.

Midway, Sandra stopped to talk with a fellow Biology student, inviting him too for a drink later. Setting off again, Sandra realised that she had forgotten the library book. Cursing her stupidity, she semi-ran back to the flat. Remembering that Margaret was asleep, Sandra entered the darkened room and, visualising the layout, picked the book off the desk where she had left it. Then she went to the library, before joining her friends for a drink in the Grassmarket.

In the early hours of the morning, when Sandra returned to her flat, she was disturbed to find several police cars and an ambulance outside the main door. After identifying herself, an officer took her up the stairs. Two things Sandra saw then will haunt her forever. The first was the blood-soaked mattress on Margaret's single bed, the second was the child-like scrawl, written with lipstick, on the dressing-table mirror, which read, 'Aren't you glad you didn't turn on the light?'

Baby Stuff

A couple from downtown Airdrie were on a well-deserved holiday in newly-fashionable Romania. One morning they were wandering round a busy market in Bucharest, their baby son sitting in the travel-sized pushchair they had brought with them. Without warning a violent argument erupted to the couple's left, with two men shouting at each other animatedly.

The innocent Airdrieonians did not realise that this was a ruse designed to distract their otherwise stalwart Caledonian attentions. Turning back to their baby boy, they found the pushchair empty. In his place sat a small bag of potatoes.

Alarmed, the couple contacted the police and a massive hunt was organised. To no avail. Despite the involvement of the British Embassy and the full co-operation of the national authorities, the joy of the young couple's life seemed to have vanished forever.

One month later a suspicious guard at the Hungarian border stopped a woman who was carrying what appeared to be a baby of incredibly pale complexion. Furthermore, on closer examination it seemed most still. Taking the woman into custody at the border post, the baby was discovered to be dead, its tiny body packed with packets of pure heroin. A funeral in Scotland was arranged shortly thereafter.

Domino Theory

It was a Mexican newspaper that first reported the fantastic new game among Royal Air Force pilots on the Falkland Islands. While undertaking reconnaissance and related activity, the airmen had noticed that when they overflow colonies of penguins, the flightless birds became awestruck by the passing fighter planes. The behaviour was similar to that of a tennis match crowd. As the planes flew one way, the penguins watched them as one; when the planes turned round, the penguins watched them return. With as many as ten thousand birds in any one colony, it was a mesmerising sight.

Things began to get interesting when the pilots flew directly over the penguins. As the birds craned their necks to watch the fly-by, their heads went back and back and back until eventually the penguins toppled over. A zoologist stationed on the islands expressed his concern about this activity to the RAF base commander. Penguins, he explained, are not good at getting up once they have fallen over. Rather than curtail his men's fun on a posting not noted for its sense of *joie de vivre*, the commanding officer hired two of the local civilians to pick the penguins up. Special gloves were required, as the birds were not always grateful to be stood up and would peck their thankless helpers.

As the pilots began to devise a scoring system, based on

ten-pin bowling, to determine who was the daily winner on the penguin run, the incensed zoologist contacted the World Wildlife Fund, who contacted the British Government. Eventually, the game was banned and the penguins left to themselves.

However, on returning to their training flights in Scotland, the Air Force were able to find a new location in the Scottish Borders to play their game.

'We can get the same effect when we fly low over Selkirk,' commented one flier, 'and most of the people seem able to pick themselves up fine, which saves us a bit of money too.'

Coatbridge Sure Thing

Coatbridge is one of those places where every night is party night. Most evenings the streets ring with the sound of convivial people of all ages enjoying liquid and spiritual merriment. There is a brisk trade in condoms.

A particularly promiscuous young chap, very much the honey for many female bees, walked into the local chemists one evening and asked for their finest brand of condom. The manager himself was on duty and was pleased to be able to provide the appropriate descriptions of the various products.

'Is this going to be a big night?' the older man inquired, himself a veteran of the town's amorous ways.

'Oh, you bet,' responded the younger man. 'Tonight is a dead certainty!'

The two then winked mischievously at each other, both relishing the cross-generational bonding.

Later that evening the younger man arrived at the home of his prospective date. She showed him in, still drying her hair, and asked that he wait in the front room. This he did. Sitting, watching the National Lottery Draw, he then heard the female say,

'Hello Dad, Steven is sitting in the front room. We'll be going out soon, though.'

Standing, Steven turned to greet the approaching father. As the man entered the room, Steven recognised him as the manager of the chemists.

Tasty Revenge

The behaviour of naughty Scottish students in London is a source of constant amusement to the local populace. Nevertheless, there are those who do not appreciate such spontaneous japery. One lad from Kelso had recently been ejected from a particular bar for suggesting that one of the bouncers would not look out of place in the primate section of the nearby zoo, although not necessarily in such words. Upset by his forcible ejection, the young man vowed revenge on the establishment, and began to foster a suitable plan with a colleague from Jedburgh.

Returning to the same bar, no one recognised the Kelso man. His head had been shorn; he was clean-shaven and looked most respectable in a cunningly obtained suit. Similarly, the Jedburgh companion looked every inch the respectable businessman.

Having settled at a table near the bar itself, the two enjoyed a few pints of beer as they waited for the venue to fill.

As soon as there were lots of people nearby, the Kelso man stood, began making retching noises and doubled up over the table. At this point he squeezed hard on a polythene bag filled with potato soup which was stuffed under his shirt. The stunned on-lookers were then treated to the sight of a highly respectable explosion of vomit over the small table.

Unable to tear their gaze away, the watching crowds then watched as the Jedburgh man reached into his breast pocket and produced a large plastic spoon, with which he proceeded to wolf down the lumpy swill dribbling all over the table.

About seven members of the public were themselves immediately sick, two staff had to be sent home and the Kelso student returned to his Kentish Town digs revenged and happy.

Well Done, Miss

The peellywally Scottish complexion is not loved by all its owners. Influenced by sophisticated television shows such as *Baywatch* and *Home and Away*, many young people seek to hide their dermatological heritage through the use of artificial aids. While in the past a fast tan could be obtained with little more than some watered-down brown sauce and a damp sponge, modern youngsters are happy to engage the latest technological aids in their quest to become sophisticated and foreign-looking.

According to the records of the local medical board, a young lady from Glasgow was eager to transform herself before her holiday in Ibiza. Having registered with one tanning shop, she was horrified to discover that there were strict limits on the number of sessions she could undertake. After only two such fifteen-minute periods, it soon became clear that it would take many months before she looked suitably foreign. Thinking quickly, and with her holiday just one week away, the woman registered with several more tanning shops, establishing a daily rota which she would undertake with the aid of the city's well-respected public transport.

All seemed to be going well. Yet after one such afternoon session, and but two days before departure, the young lady began to notice a strange smell, seemingly coming through her pores. The situation worsened on the bus home, as other passengers averted their noses as if in the presence of something foul, an attitude the woman's family were happy to repeat. Distraught, she headed for the local medical practice who, alarmed at her tale, referred her immediately to the nearest hospital. There, the incredulous house staff listened to her tale while awaiting results of the x-ray they had taken – an x-ray that confirmed that the young lady had but hours to live, having slowly cooked her own intestines over the past seven days.

Tay Mind-scanner

One of the many psychics for which Dundee is well known began to get messages of uncanny directness. Compared to her usual visions, these were of remarkable clarity. The only discomforting aspect was that most of the details within these other-worldly communications concerned criminal or similar activities.

Worn down by a sense of guilt, the psychic decided to tell the police. By nature sceptical, the detective concerned followed up the first such lead and was delighted to thwart the robbery of a suburban DIY shop. Buoyed up by this success, the psychic and the police were soon at work on the next potential crime, and the next, and the next.

As word spread of their supernatural success, the psychic began to receive telephone calls from police forces all over Scotland. Yet strangely, her record of achievement never seemed to extend beyond the city boundaries of Dundee. Nevertheless, word spread of the Dundonian police's secret tool and it was not long before local and national media began to pay an interest in the city's 'psychic Kojak'.

After arriving at the lady's home for an exclusive interview, a national television company began to wire themselves in for a high-profile piece of broadcasting. They had not been in the house for more than one hour when the sound engineer reported strange noises on all of his several microphones. On closer examination these noises were traced to the house's antiquated heating system. On closer examination still, these noises were shown to be conversations from a nearby house, relayed along the old pipes.

Subsequent investigations revealed that the house in question was the den of a local crime syndicate. In one puff of acoustic logic the psychic's credibility was destroyed, leaving her to return to the drab living-rooms of so many widows and widowers desperate to contact their departed loved ones.

No Smoke

A businessman from just outside Motherwell went to Cuba with his wife, hoping to catch the flavour of the nation before the end of the Castro regime. Having sated himself on sun and sand, and disappointed at the lack of golf courses, the man decided to take advantage of the local produce, purchasing an exceptionally expensive box of cigars.

On returning to his countryside home, the canny businessman realised that his pricey Havana cigars would benefit from insurance; against fire, theft, loss and so on. Within a month, having smoked his entire stockpile of these great cigars and without yet having made even his premium payment on the policy, the man filed a claim against the insurance company. In it he explained in writing that the cigars had been lost in 'a series of small fires'. For obvious reasons, the Edinburgh-based company refused to pay, noting that the cigars 'had been consumed in the customary manner'. Unperturbed, the man took the matter to the courts . . . and won. The sheriff concerned agreed with the insurance company that the original claim was 'deceptive'. Nevertheless, he also stated that the man held a policy from the company in which it was made quite clear that the cigars were insurable, that they could be insured against fire, and that at no point did the documentation make clear what a 'legitimate fire' was.

As such they had no choice but to pay out. Rather than take on a costly and potentially embarrassing appeal, the company accepted this initial ruling, handing over several thousand pounds in compensation for the lost cigars.

Shortly after the cheque was cashed, there was a knock at the man's elegant front door. Two police officers arrested him on 12 counts of arson. With the use of his own written insurance claim and testimony from the original court case being used against him, a different sheriff convicted the man of deliberately burning his own property, sentencing him to 12 months in jail and a £10,000 fine. Although the jail term was suspended on appeal, as a result of his conviction the man was barred from holding any directorships and subsequently lost control of his own business. Two years later he was homeless and divorced. When last heard of, a placement for teacher training in northern England had just been secured.

One Careful Owner

Aberdonians pride themselves on their intense appreciation of money and are ever eager to seek out the bargains that most of us might miss. Aberdonian students are in many respects the ultimate bargain-seeking machines, leaving few supermarket noticeboards unscanned in their search for the almost-free. Yet even the most canny bargain hunter would have been suspicious of the advert that one student from the Granite City found while perusing the 'For Sale' column in his Edinburgh digs:

'Porsche For Sale. As New. Soft Top. All Extras. Black, leather interior. £50.'

Thinking this a mistake, the Aberdonian nevertheless felt it necessary to check, borrowing his flatmate's mobile phone while she slept, and calling the number listed. A sultry New Town Edinburgh voice confirmed the details listed, then hung up. Stopping only to make several more calls on his chum's phone, the student set off for the address given, armed with £50 and a sense of optimistic disbelief. Arriving at the appropriate mews house, the door was opened by an attractive, middle-aged brunette, who led the young man straight into the attached garage. There, just as described in the advertisement, was the Porsche.

Still somewhat incredulous, the student paced round the vehicle, remembering his mother's advice to be wary of people from the capital and their cosmopolitan ways. Yet sensing nothing strange about the car, £50 was handed over. Prior to driving off, the student felt compelled to stop and ask for the full story on the vehicle.

'Well,' said the brunette, counting ten-pound notes into a white envelope, 'the car originally belonged to my husband. That is to say, my ex-husband. A few months back he confessed to having an affair with my best friend. I was very upset but have now come to terms with it.

'Anyway, the other day I get a phone call from him. He and my friend are looking to put a deposit down on a new house, and since I'd been so understanding about the whole thing, he asked if there was a favour I could do him.

'"Sure," I said.

'"Oh, thank you so much," he said. "I was wondering, do you think you could sell my Porsche and send me half the money?"'

And with that, she licked the envelope and sealed it.

Kilmarnock Nativity Variation

The performance of the school nativity play in Kilmarnock is an annual source of parental joy. Tickets always sell out well in advance. Competition among the children for the best parts is stiff, with campaigns for selection often beginning in the early days of autumn.

One year the competition was more fierce than usual. After many auditions and reviews, the part of Joseph went to a young boy called James, to the intense excitement of both James and his family. Yet rehearsals had barely started before it became clear that James was having problems. Perhaps star struck by having such a big role, the young boy was unable to master any of his lines. Despite private tuition from the drama teacher, no amount of coaching could rectify his halted, stumbling delivery.

After much deliberation in the staff room, it was decided to switch James with the boy who was playing the innkeeper, a much smaller, less prestigious role. Although James took the news very badly, he nevertheless agreed to the switch. Yet as rehearsals continued, his grumpiness seemed to grow.

On the night itself everything went according to the director's meticulous instructions. Staff and parents sat enraptured as the miniature Joseph and Mary made their way towards Bethlehem. Arriving at the cardboard inn door, they knocked three times. Slowly the door was pulled open by an innkeeper who appeared much happier than he had in rehearsals.

'Is there any room at the inn for us?' asked Joseph, right on cue.

'Well,' said the diminutive innkeeper, 'there's certainly somewhere for Mary, but Joseph can piss off.'

A Farewell to Arms

The beautiful countryside of the Scottish Lowlands is a good persuader when it comes to relaxation. An American tourist, over to trace his ancestors, was making his way around the rolling hills of Melrose. The streaming daylight and the fresh country air had moved the man into a state of euphoric intoxication, his genes swaying in time to the ancient harmonies of the old country.

So complete was his reverie, and so loud was the music of traditional Scottish origin on his in-car CD player, that he entirely failed to notice how closely he would pass by an agricultural container on one of the area's notoriously thin roads. Thus his right arm, swaying in the breeze through the wound-down window, was ripped from its socket by the metal side of the truck. It was not until another motorist noticed the bloody stump protruding from the car that the American was alerted to his injury. The persistent horn blare woke him from his inner journey, whereupon he noticed his woeful state. The doctor at the local hospital was amazed that the tourist had no recollection of any incident. The limb was never recovered.

Good Plan

A loving old couple in Inverness had been together for many years. Though both were sound of spirit, their minds were somewhat removed from the day to day aspects of life. Driving into town one Saturday afternoon, it was agreed that the husband would wait in the car while his wife went into the supermarket for the few groceries she needed. As he waved her goodbye, the old man turned on the radio to listen to the sport, settling back comfortably in his string-beaded seat.

One hour later his wife had completed her shopping and, forgetting entirely about the waiting car, hopped on the bus. Arriving at their home, she thought little of the absence of her husband, presuming him to be out for a drive. But by tea-time, when he had still not returned, she was growing anxious and telephoned the police. It was fully one day later that the car was found, the radio silent, the battery dead and the sleeping elderly gentleman quite unable to remember what he was doing there.

Management Bonus

The quiet villages surrounding Edinburgh are home to many of the city's high-powered financial people. Taking the train into work, and walking the short distances from Waverley Station to their swish offices, is preferable to negotiating the capital's infamously congested streets.

One financial adviser, an employee at a top insurance company, had been out to lunch with an important client. Having enjoyed a beautiful meal, the client had insisted that they continue to enjoy themselves at a number of pubs, a distressing task that the financial adviser undertook with dutiful vigour. By five o'clock both were intoxicated in the extreme. As the client announced that he needed to go back to his hotel, the financial adviser took his leave gratefully and made for the train station.

The journey away from Edinburgh was not pleasant. That evening the train was particularly full and the financial adviser was forced to stand in the middle of a busy, sweaty carriage, with other passengers pressing in on him from all around. The train seemed to sway more dynamically than usual. Soon, the financial adviser knew he was going to be sick.

Unable to make his way to either the bathroom or the window, he seized his briefcase from the overhead rack, bent down to the floor as if looking for papers, and emptied the slushy contents of his stomach into it. He then put the case back on the rack and continued the journey, substantially more at ease than before.

Coming to the next day, he remembered with horror the events of the journey home. Downstairs he could hear his wife making up the dainty sandwiches he preferred. Rushing to prevent her placing them in his briefcase, he grabbed the offending item and took it into the bathroom, intending to empty out its less pleasant contents. Clicking the case open, he found only his morning paper from the previous day and some files from the office. Stunned, he realised that he had not been sick in his own briefcase.

Wrong Club

Some golf courses are more testing than others. Outside Glasgow there is one renowned, and exclusive, course which is as difficult as it is famous. Flanked at several parts by a body of water, people travel from around the world to play its much-televised fairways.

Coming to terms with the course's level of difficulty is not easy for some. Having looked forward to gaining access to it for so long, being humiliated is difficult to swallow. One golfer, patient for many a year, was finally rewarded with a tee-time for him and his three colleagues. Although a keen and ambitious golfer already, much practice was taken beforehand to ensure a successful debut.

The day was a disaster. From the moment that the man stepped on to the course, he was unable to find his shots. His grip on the clubs became over-loose, his judgement of the distances proved ridiculous, his stance fell apart. From tee to green, everything that could go wrong did. For him. For his colleagues, their golf was as satisfying as the weather was pleasant.

Ultimately, this imbalance of fortunes took its toll. Seizing his golf clubs, the man marched to the nearby water and threw the leather bag into the depths, before striding off towards the car park. Astonished at this turn of events, his companions were pleased to see him walking back towards them five minutes later. Clearly common sense had prevailed. Those were, after all, expensive clubs. Sure enough, their friend walked straight past them and into the waters, without stopping to remove shoes or trousers. Thrashing around wildly, he found the thrown bag and hauled it to the shore. He then unzipped the front pocket, removed his car keys and threw the bag back into the loch.

Perth Satellite Result

A joiner in Perth was enjoying some satellite television football in one of the quaint town's many pubs. Although his own team was not playing, the team in similar colours was winning, and a good time was being had by all. When it came to the end of the match, most remained to discuss the finer points of the game, and much fun was had at the expense of the referee. By the time it came for all to go home, the joiner was almost helplessly convivial, and had to be urged on his way by a couple of the cheery barstaff.

Wandering back to his house, the joiner felt the drink hitting his sensibility like a train, forcing him to debate the whereabouts of the street he lived on. At times sitting down to consider his position, it at some point became absolutely clear that the best thing to do was to have a lie down and think about things. This he did.

Awakening several hours later, as the first twinkle of a beautiful Tay day was appearing on the horizon, the joiner found himself unable to move. Slowly, through a deafening, painful fog of alcohol, he realised that he had chosen to lie down on an area of the pavement that had just been repaired. While he had slept, the concrete had hardened. Although he was eventually chipped out by some workmen, he was several hours late for work.

Imprisoned Tourist

A visit to the homeland of her tartan ancestors had long been the dream of an elderly American female from Ohio. Newly retired, and rich from the sale of the agricultural store where she had toiled for thirty years, the proud Scot booked her passage. Landing at a foggy Edinburgh International Airport late on a Sunday night, a limousine was awaiting her from the top-notch establishment hotel she was booked into.

Two bright eyes peered through the glass at the mysterious country around her.

Arriving at the hotel the lady was thrilled to find the car door being opened by a kilted gentleman, who said something in suitably brusque tones. Looking around, she was able to make out the silhouette of the castle, nuzzling the sky.

Escorted with refined obsequiousness to her luxury room, the staff of the hotel were pleased as ever to help such an enthusiastic visitor to Scotland, even though they themselves were Spanish.

One hour later the telephone rang at the front desk. The skilfully polite receptionist answered. The distressed voice of the American lady came down the line.

'I'm trapped in my room!' she exclaimed.

'How do you mean, "trapped", madam?' enquired the receptionist.

'There's no way I can get out!' came the voice.

'Can you see a door?'

'Yes.'

'Then please go through it, madam.'

'It's only the bathroom,' the panicked voice announced.

'Is there another door, madam?' asked the smooth service operative.

'Yes, but I can't go through that one. I'm trapped!'

'Why can't you go through that one, Madam?'

'Because it's got a sign on it saying "Do Not Disturb"!'

Snap Decision

A wealthy publican from Crieff was most proud of his Ferrari. There were no others quite like it; electric blue, with yellow leather seats, it was the very model of stylish success he had been looking for. He loved nothing better than to whiz around the surrounding country roads, feeling his masculine prowess oozing from every pore of the bespoke upholstery.

It was on one such night-time drive that the publican was caught by a new camera-based speedtrap. He did not realise it at the time and was shocked to receive a fine in the post a few days later, complete with a photographic image of his car, zooming along at significantly over the regulation speed. The letter demanded immediate payment of a hefty fine.

Making light of the matter, the man duly wrote out a cheque for the required amount, took a photograph of it and sent the photograph back to the authorities.

'If it's good enough for them, then it's good enough for me,' he boasted to a spellbound back bar of drinkers.

The publican's joviality took a downturn when, two days later, another envelope arrived from the authorities. This one contained a photograph of a police cell.

A real cheque was dispatched by return post.

Star-struck Cone Incident

Sometimes, on those odd occasions when it rains, there's not much to do in Scotland. The cinema is an obvious escape. After many years of devotion to the big screen, a Scots lassie was having her first ever visit to the United States of America. She had long fantasised about going to California, and in particular about seeing one or two of her Hollywood idols. Having won a competition in her local multiplex based on monthly popcorn consumption, this was a dream come true.

With a full bag of luggage and plenty advice from her parents, the young lady was seen off at the airport by most of her village and two members of the local media.

After a hectic couple of days spent trailing round Los Angeles, peering through the bars of the celebrity homes, the young lady went down to the seaside area of Santa Monica, in the hope of catching a glimpse of a true superstar.

After hours of wandering fruitlessly along the beach, she popped into an ice-cream parlour to have a cooling snack. Then her dream came true. There, standing at the counter, was none other than David Hasselhof, looking incredibly A-list. Finding herself almost unable to speak, the woman paid for the ice-cream and left.

Standing outside the shop, it was a couple of moments before her natural instincts crept in and the young lady realised that she had forgotten her ice-cream cone. Approaching the counter again, she enquired about what had happened to her purchase.

'If you take a look, madam,' the shop assistant advised, 'you'll find it's in your handbag, where you put it a minute ago.'

Constantinople Side-effect

A fast-paced media-type couple from high-flying metro-politan Glasgow had booked an exotic holiday as part of their scheduled quality down-time. Neither of them had been to Istanbul and the opportunity to do so on a high-priced four-day elite package was more than they could resist. Wishing to ensure that their own time was truly relaxing, they had gained the services of the husband's obliging mother to babysit for their two-year-old son while they were away.

On the morning of their flight, with only a few minutes to go before their taxi arrived, the couple were concerned that the mother had still not arrived. With a car waiting outside to take them to the airport, they telephoned the nearby house to check that she was on her way. She was not. Reading the paper in front of the fire, the mother had dozed off. Alerted by their call, she told them to get on their way and that she would be round in only a minute, and would let herself in with her keys.

The couple enjoyed a fabulous break in Turkey. They were able to relax totally. On their return, they discovered the body of their son in his cot, where they had left him. The doctor diagnosed a combination of starvation and dehydration. The mother, it turned out, was also dead. The heart attack she suffered moments after rushing to put her coat on was probably due to panic.

Dunfermline Pamela

The firemen and women of Dunfermline are used to being called out for all manner of non-fire related rescues. Being good-natured types, they understand their community role. So when the call occasionally comes to help with an animal in distress, they are happy to oblige.

One such visit involved a small cat called Pamela who was stuck in a tree. Her elderly owner was distraught. Arriving at the old oak, the fire crew soon had their ladders up and in a matter of moments their most senior cat expert was coaxing the timid creature along the branch. Within ten minutes of their arrival, cat and owner were tearfully united. Delirious with joy, the old lady offered everyone tea and some home-made millionaire's shortbread, which the gallant rescuers were happy to accept, there being no pressing calls.

Climbing back into their cab, the crew gave a farewell 'Wow! Wow!' on the fire engine siren, and then ran over Pamela, who was sleeping under the rear right wheel.

Curry Night

No night out in Elgin is complete without a visit to one of its famous curry houses, to which people travel from all over the Highlands in search of that joyful burning feeling. One farmer from a holding just outside Rothes was a particular fan of tandoori chicken, and would journey to the nearby town whenever time and income allowed. Naturally, during the lambing season, there was little opportunity for any such visits. Thus it was the case that the farmer would seek to reward himself with a curry of exceptional quality on the day when lambing was completed.

One year the season had been particularly tough, with all manner of strange diseases to contend with. As a result, the farmer had to delay his celebratory curry by a week or so, by which time he was famished in a way no non-curry fans can ever imagine. Finally the night came. Everything was arranged. A local hire car would pick him up from his cottage and transport him along the winding road to Elgin. An 'extra-special' reservation had been made at one of the finest curry houses there is. Most importantly, the proprietors had been informed that they were to make this the hottest tandoori chicken that they could, without altogether subverting the taste with mere heat.

Arriving at the establishment, the farmer was greeted with a welcoming pint of lager, and then another and another. When the tandoori chicken came out from the kitchen, the farmer's mouth began to water almost uncontrollably. No sooner had the fiery dish been sat down than he was wolfing his way through it, delighting in the intensity of its power. More lager accompanied this.

Dropped off at home some few hours later by the same local hire car, the farmer was beginning to feel the effect of his indulgence. A regular sufferer from hemorrhoids, in his drunken state he mistook the effect of the exceptionally hot curry. Dashing into his bathroom, the farmer ripped down his trousers and began scrabbling in the cabinet under the sink for the hemorrhoid cream he often used to alleviate the ailment. Finding the tube, he hastily applied the ointment, lathering it on with his right hand with an air of profound relief. Yet as he did so, he experienced no diminishing in the pain he felt. Nor, for some reason, could he remove his hand. Raising the tube to his eyes, he found that, rather than the desired hemorrhoid cream, he had in fact applied instant bathroom sealant, a super-strong adhesive used in plumbing, and in so doing had joined both his buttocks and hand in an unusual and uncomfortable triumvirate.

Last Bus Home

Five English students studying in Edinburgh were determined to live up to the locals' estimation of them as lovable, high-spirited jesters. Having been out for most of the night enjoying beer at cheap prices in one of the hilarious, wacky pubs which are designed to appeal to their puerile tastes, the group were intent on home and a few games of Twister.

It being Friday night, the desire for taxis far exceeded supply, and with no sign of any of the daytime buses with which they were familiar, the five seemed to have no alternative but to walk home.

Passing the bus terminus, one of them had a brainwave. Why not steal a bus and drive home in that? How hilarious, everyone agreed. With that they put down the traffic cones they were carrying to show how wacky and alternative they were, and climbed into the depot. One hour later a number 41 bus was roaring out, transporting them back to the student ghetto of Marchmont.

The bunch of them were easily caught. The closed-circuit recording from the depot revealed them in full detail, running around the enormous building, in such a way and for such a length of time that their faces and clothes were recorded from every angle and with great precision. When questioned by the police about why they had taken so long to steal the bus, and in so doing, lost any chance to get away with it, the leader of the group was innocently revealing.

'Yeah, well, it took us a long time to find a number 41.'

Hello?

While new technology solves problems for many, for the few it presents seemingly unfathomable problems. A Cumbernauld bank robber had a routine of driving up into the less suspecting areas of the country and presenting himself at bank tellers' windows in smaller towns, with a note demanding money. With the closure of so much of the rural banking network, the man found his potential targets diminishing in size. At the same time he was also aware of the increasing number of automatic banking machines. Sensing a new opportunity, he approached one of these autotellers with the same note he had been using in his previous bank heists. Tapping the screen of the machine, he held the note up for the man inside to read. When, after a few further taps, there was no response, he began to tap more loudly, shouting into the tiny slot. He was still shouting when the police came to take him away.

Fishy Sales

One year the salmon harvest was not up to scratch. The industry was in turmoil – the meat from the fish was not the right colour. Rather than the usual delicious-looking pink, that season's returns had about them a paler, almost white complexion.

Although actually tastier than the usual fare, there could still be no doubt that the average consumer would not be happy with the change of hue. Then a bright young man in marketing came up with a simple solution. Each and every tin of salmon produced that year had on it the over-printed legend, 'Guaranteed Not to Turn Pink in the Tin'. An important part of the economy was saved overnight.

Road Hazard

There remain those who would still drink and drive, despite the heavy penalties and potential for tragedy. A white-collar man from around the Grampians was a habitual drink-driver, despite the constant admonishments of his fearful family. One typically inglorious morning the man's dutiful wife came downstairs and found her dishevelled husband asleep on the kitchen floor, the air above him reeking of beer.

Woken with a shove, the man leaped up and into the shower, bursting out three minutes later for a hasty shave and the scramble for a clean shirt. As he burst past her for the front door, his wife had enough time to think that she needed him to pick up some groceries on the way home. Running out to catch him, she caught sight of the car reversing out of the garage, her sweating husband at the wheel, and the body of a small child impacted on the radiator grill.

Falkirk Rover

The staff at the Animal Welfare Centre in Falkirk were not particularly concerned to get a call from a man saying that he and his family were no longer able to look after Rover. Unwanted pets are a common, if unfortunate, occurrence. The volunteer who took the call asked if the family could bring the Rover in, but the caller suggested that the pet was now beyond control. A van and a man were sent out to complete the job.

Ringing the bell at the pebble-dashed terraced house, the door was opened by a frightened-looking little girl, who beckoned the animal man inside. Wordlessly, she pointed upstairs.

Arriving at the top landing, the man found the father, mother and son standing outside a closed door.

'How old is Rover?' the rescuer asked, trying to tone down the tense atmosphere.

'Ten, we think,' said the mother.

At that the man opened the door and went in to find a large crocodile sitting by the window. The man reached for his mobile telephone.

After capture, the man-eating reptile was eventually found a home with a zoo in northern England. The father was unable to pinpoint exactly where he had got the crocodile, other than something about 'a man in Polmont'. The seller was never found.

Compulsive Viewing

The night was drawing to a close in a small village in Scotland. For hours the family had watched a succession of prime-time television, culminating in the news. The young son had pleaded with his mother and father to be allowed to stay up and watch the late film. Finally relenting, they all settled back for two hours of schlock horror mayhem.

As the final credits rolled, the boy's parents realised that it had been a long time since their son had uttered a word. Looking over at him, his eyes appeared lifeless, focused entirely on the flicker of the screen. After calling his name several times, the father was horrified to release that his son appeared to be in some form of trance, unable to speak and oblivious to all stimulation.

With the house in alarm, the local doctor was called, who declined the family's urges to 'give their son something' to recover normal consciousness. Instead, the wise doctor asked the family to recount what had happened that evening. The bemused father explained quickly how the night had progressed. The doctor asked if the family possessed a video camera. When they said that they did, the doctor then asked for it to be linked up to the television. Having completed this link-up, the doctor then took the video camera, trained it on the father's fearful face, and told him to tell his son that it was time to go to bed. Upon doing as instructed, the son dutifully got up and went to bed.

In the morning he was back in front of the television, awaiting further instruction. The doctor advised that they should continue the treatment for a week or so, instructing the child to 'go outside and play' and 'make friends' but never to watch television. Ten days later the son had not only returned to normality, he was a brighter, happier child, who never watched television again.

Going Down

On a visit to Aberdeen for a two-day training course in stock control, a management trainee from Perth was staying in one of the Granite City's less plush hotels. Tired from that afternoon's session, the young lady had gone to her room to have a rest before the evening's 'networking' session. Drifting off under the tired light of a 40-watt bulb, the delegate from Perth became ensnared in a terrible nightmare, the likes of which she had never before suffered.

In this dream she saw an ice-cream van pulling up outside the hotel, its bell ringing loudly. As she walked towards the van, its service shutter was pulled sharply up, revealing a white-suited man with a terrible pock-marked face and a worn copy of the Bible. Snarling, this man then jumped out of the van, dropping the book and pulling a large knife from his jacket.

Startled awake, the Perth woman caught her breath and then showered. A fellow trainee called to arrange to meet her so that they and some others might go downstairs together.

This small group met at the elevator. As the doors slid open, the woman from Perth was shocked to find a man already in the lift with the same pock-marked face she had seen in her nightmare. Stumbling back, she declined to step through the doors, pretending that some necessary item had been left behind in her room.

It was just as she was putting the key into the lock of her room that the trainee felt the thunderous crash of the elevator hitting the bottom of the lift shaft, killing all those inside. No body of a pock-marked man was ever found.

Interrupted
Wishaw Courtship Session

A courting couple from Wishaw were abroad at night and looking for somewhere to park the car and enjoy their own comforts. Finding an undistinguished farm track, they drove along it. After a hundred yards or so they came to a peaceful glade, wherein they set about each other with relish, to the musical accompaniment of the late-night romantic slot of a well-respected national radio station.

At a point that could probably be described as 'halfway', the couple's love was interrupted by an urgent news report, explaining that a madman had escaped from a nearby mental institution. Staring around them into the darkness, both agreed on the terror of the situation. But when the man attempted to start the car, the engine would not fire. Again and again he turned the key but to no positive outcome. Eventually he decided to get out and go for help, instructing his companion to lock the doors and not to open them under any circumstances.

It was nearly ten full petrifying minutes before the woman saw the approaching blue lights. At the same time she heard the sound of banging on the roof of the car. Yet she was not so scared now. Soon she was surrounded by police cars and armed police. A loudhailer instructed her to get out and run to the nearest officer, and under no circumstances to look back.

Thrusting the door open, she burst out but was unable to stop herself looking at the top of the car, where a wild man dressed in a red tracksuit was banging her boyfriend's head off the metal roof.

Chip-based Justice

A family man from the East Neuk of Fife had reached the end of his tether. Unable to provide for his wife and children through the skills in which he had been trained, he felt no option but to resort to crime. Being something of an amateur, he decided to start with smaller establishments and work his way up.

His first choice was a fish and chip shop in Pittenweem. Arriving with a plastic gun and Balaclava, the family man demanded the contents of the till. Yet as he was standing there, the smell of delicious fish and chips was too much to resist, so he also demanded a couple of fish suppers to take away and a wee poke of chips for now – 'Plenty of salt and sauce, please.'

As he turned to leave, with the takings from the shop in a plastic bag, one of his lovely chips dropped out of its carton and landed on the floor, whereupon the man slipped on it, concussing himself against the wall on the way down.

As the proprietor of the fish and chip shop told the *Pittenweem Tribune*, 'It's not the first time that a thief has been caught because they were unable to resist the allure of our famous foodstuffs.'

Admissible Evidence

While never condoned, the presence of drink-driving in rural settings is perhaps an inevitable result of combining isolation with desperation. A man from a small village near Forres did not intend to drink and drive when the evening started, but the presence of a bad wind and the absence of a good friend took its effect.

After a heavy session in one of the Highland town's better value inns, he climbed into his Toyota and set off. About midway between bar and home, a police patrol spotted his car weaving back and forth across the road at about 10 m.p.h. As they were approaching a corner of notorious danger, the policemen overtook swiftly and ushered the errant motorist into the side of the road, where he sat, fearing and knowing the worst. Seeking absolution, he opened the door, dropped to his knees and began to pray as the silhouette of an officer of the law with breathalyser kit approached. Just then there was the squeal of an overworked engine and hurtling towards the corner came an old Morris Marina, piloted by an equally inebriated drinking chum of the man on his knees.

Taken aback by the tableaux of penitence before him, the Morris Marina man hurtles into the corner with inadequate care, disappearing through the fence and down a steep embankment. Immediately the two police officers dash off after him. Simultaneously worried about his friend but thrilled with the opportunity, the man on his knees jumps up and into the car, and careers off in the direction of home. Arriving back, he parks in the garage with expert care, before running inside to awaken his wife. Explaining to her the situation in brief, he demands her loyalty. Meekly, she agrees.

Two hours later, during which time both have been lying awake in bed, there is the sound of a car approaching, then a knock on the door. Clad in pyjamas, husband and wife open the door to the two policemen. Professing complete ignorance of any of the night's events and expressing absolute concern at the news of their friend's accident, both contend that the husband has been at home all evening.

'We watched a film and then the news,' the wife says.

'*The Great Escape*,' the husband expands. 'Again.'

Everybody smiles. Apparently happy with the story they have been told, the policemen ask whether, for the sake of good order, they might take a look at the man's car – 'You know, just for our report.'

Eager to please, the couple walk with the officers to the garage where, upon opening the door and turning the light on, they find themselves contemplating a white police car complete with fluorescent stripes.

'What have you been up to?' asks the man, turning to his spouse.

Right of Passage

The seas around Scotland are often home to various NATO exercises. On one occasion a small armada of ships of many sizes had converged off the West Coast to engage in a series of mock battles. After the conclusion of one of the scenarios, all ships were instructed to rendez-vous at a certain point near the Inner Hebrides.

With a heavy fog enveloping the area, the airwaves were alive with every manner of signals, all much appreciated by the wargame enthusiasts who like to tune in, quite illegally, to military broadcasts. One such hobbyist recorded the following exchange.

Radio 1: Please divert your course 20 degrees to the South as you are on a collision course.

Radio 2: Recommend you divert *your* course.

Radio 1: Please divert your course 20 degrees to the South to avoid a collision.

Radio 2: Recommend you divert *your* course.

Radio 1 [new voice]: This is the captain of a US Navy ship. Divert, repeat, divert your course now.

Radio 2: No, I say again, no – divert *your* course.

Radio 1: We are an aircraft carrier of the US Navy. We are a large warship. Divert your course now!

Radio 2: This is a lighthouse. You decide.

Note of Thanks

A young mother was having trouble with her gaggle of unruly children as they departed the supermarket. The bedlam continued as they climbed into the family car parked on a nearby street, with children bouncing up and down repeatedly on the seats, the car filled with noise. Passers-by watched amusedly as the clearly rattled mother set about trying to get out of her tight parking space, the children still wailing and shouting as she did so.

Unsurprisingly, the car reversed hard into the brand new sports car parked behind it, denting the shiny bonnet. The onlookers gasped. Applying the handbrake sharply and stopping the car without further ado, the mother got out and inspected the damage. Going back to her car, she returned with a pen and paper, with which she wrote the following note, to the evident satisfaction of her street-side audience.

'To whom it may concern. I'm having a crap day and hitting your smug new sports car just made it worse. Everyone around thinks I'm writing some sort of apology and giving you my contact details. But I'm not.'

Wrong Number

It was a pleasant evening in early autumn, and the Stirling university lecturer and his lawyer wife had hired a female student to babysit while they attended a choral concert. The student arrived promptly and, after being shown all over the house, assured the young parents that there was no need to worry; that everything would be fine – their three-year-old daughter was in safe hands.

Suitably assured, the couple left and the student settled down to a quiet night in a nice house with a good book. After half an hour she popped upstairs to check on the sleeping child but there was no need for concern. Returning downstairs, she had just settled back into her book when the telephone rang. Lifting the receiver, she heard only some heavy breathing. Disgusted, she slammed the telephone down, only for it to ring again immediately. This time, a harsh male voice informed her with undisguised longing that he intended to enter the house and kill both her and the child. After ringing off, the student called the police and explained what had happened. A sympathetic officer took down all the relevant details and told her to stay put until a police car arrived, noting that they would be monitoring the telephone line for future threats.

No sooner had she replaced the telephone and triple-locked all the windows and doors, than the telephone rang again. Putting the handset gently to her ear, she listened aghast as the same male voice now explained in great detail exactly how he intended to kill her. At that point the excited voice of the police officer came on the line.

'Get out! He's on another extension somewhere in the house!' But it was already too late.

Deliverance from Above

Returning one night from a promotional evening at a nearby Thai restaurant, a young Penicuik couple opened the door to their detached house. Before them was the severely crushed body of their dead dog; above them a circular hole in the roof; and all around a foul-smelling substance of unknown origin. Distressed, they immediately called the police, who arrived and sealed off the area. It was several days before the true story emerged.

A passing 747 jet had encountered a large pocket of turbulence which had caused the toilet waste container to explode, the vile matter within freezing into a hard block as it plummeted from 37,000 feet. This putrid boulder impacted at tremendous velocity into the house, creating a bullet-like hole in the roof before finally crushing the helpless hound. Some time after, the ball melted, reverting to its putrid room-temperature form, rendering the house uninhabitable. The young couple refused to return to the previously highly desirable property and it was demolished. They never bought another dog.

Convenient Position

A West Coast hospital had a problem with one of its beds. Rumour had spread that the bed in question was haunted. Even among staff there was a general feeling of unease. No other reason could be found to explain why the past three occupants of the bed had all died, despite being in a state of recovery rather than remission. The entire ward had been checked for any sign of infection, with all of the air vents being thoroughly cleaned, while the bed itself had been turned over from top to bottom for evidence of any possible cause. There was nothing.

Following all of the requested reports, the hospital's chief administrator then had all of the relevant nursing staff quizzed heavily. None could provide any explanation and none seemed to have done anything wrong.

Puzzled, the chief administrator found herself on the ward in the early hours of the morning, supervising the arrival of the next patient for the bed and determined that nothing should befall this new occupant.

Just as the sedated patient had been placed in the bed, the cleaner arrived and began to set himself up for a floor polishing session. The chief administrator immediately intervened, stopping the cleaner in his linoleum tracks. It was later documented how, in order to make the flex of his floor polisher reach from one end of the ward to the other, the cleaner had started to use a particular wall socket, the same wall socket into which the supposedly haunted bed's life support system was always plugged.

Dumbarton Conundrum

While Dumbarton is generally a peaceable community of national envy, the local constabulary were aware of a sudden and seemingly inexplicable rise in the number of car thefts. Unable to handle this development with any degree of conviction, a senior detective was summoned from Glasgow to assist. No sooner had the sharp-eyed female arrived, than she asked to see details of all the cars involved.

'Most of these are red,' she noted.

Wide-eyed with wonder at her big-city forensic ways, the Dumbarton police concurred with this evidence, whereupon the detective asked for a watch to be kept on all of the city's yellow cars.

With astonishing speed, a group of youths were arrested the following night breaking into a yellow car. Amazed, the local media asked for an explanation.

'We've had this in Glasgow,' she noted, climbing into her fast sports car. 'People get bored with simple car theft and need something else to amuse themselves. Basically, they were playing a form of snooker using car colours.'

Stunned at this revelation, everyone stepped back and watched as the ingenious woman drove off into the distance.

Paisley Night In

A young woman from Paisley was enjoying a non-stop night of salubrious inebriation at one of her chum's houses when she became worn down with intoxication and decided to seek respite in a darkened bedroom. Some hours later the girl found herself having a terrible nightmare, as the town's landmarks and roads whizzed by her head at an eerie speed, causing her to scream. These same screams caused the car on which she was lying to stop.

It later became clear how, when near blind with alcohol, the woman had entered, not the darkened bedroom that she had perceived, but the connected garage of the semi-detached house. And her friend's father had not noticed her prostrate body when he set off for his job at the railway station. The young woman gave up drink with immediate, but not permanent, effect.

Good Lesson

Lecturers at Glasgow University are among the finest in the land and excel in the field of practical instruction. At an opening session for first year biochemistry students, one of the department's most admired academics began to explain the importance of the sense of taste, with particular regard to diabetes.

To do so the lecturer first asked one of the students to provide a urine sample. With much sniggering from his classmates, a chap from Musselburgh obliged behind the curtain to one side of the room.

The lecturer then dipped her finger into the sample jar, before opening her mouth and taking a good suck on it. She explained that by so doing it was possible to determine the sugar content of the sample. The woman then invited all the students to come down and repeat what she had done. Fearing failure, all did so, trotting uneasily up to the not-too-pleasant container one by one.

Once the students had sat down again, the lecturer asked them to observe very closely while she repeated her demonstration. With deliberate slowness, she dipped her index finger into the urine, while licking from her middle finger. The point she was making concerned the importance of observation rather than taste.

Although several of the class were immediately sick, none forgot the lesson.

Constant Companion

A large group of retirees from Chicago, all of Scottish descent, had booked a touring holiday to Scotland. Their first port of call was Inverness and a visit to the nearby Loch, whereby some would stand gazing out in search of the monster while others in the group took their photographs.

Moments before their tour guide called them back to the bus, several members of the group noticed an old man standing near the water's edge. Clad in traditional Highland dress he was in every respect the quintessential tourist image of a Scot, and all there were keen to capture him for their photo albums. Although many of the group attempted to engage the elderly chap in conversation, he responded to their talk with nothing but a weary glare, before returning to look over the waters.

A similar scene occurred at the nearby Castle Urquhart. Just as the group was departing – having run their hands repeatedly over the ruined walls of the once proud fortress – several of them spotted the same old man in Highland dress. Although they called and waved, still his only response was a glance in their direction of mild but unmistakable disdain.

The tour then made its way down to Dunfermline and its historic abbey. Here the group was treated to a wonderful wander around what was for many years the centre of the Scottish monarchy. On nearing the end of this instructive walk, the Americans were amazed to see the old man from Castle Urquhart watching them from the shadow of a nearby grave. Waving, they approached him as they would a lost relative. Still he refused to converse, merely nodding his head in their direction, his hand resting on the erect stone before him.

On the final day of their holiday the coach pulled into the car park at the entrance of Edinburgh Castle. As the final point in their whirlwind visit, none of them could have wished for more. Over and around the magnificent landmark they roamed, eager to visit every dungeon, stateroom and cupboard. No sooner had they come upon the famous cannon Mons Meg than they spied a familiar figure watching them. There was the old Highlander, clad in the same Highland wear, considering all around him with an eye that burned with worldly cynicism.

Knowing that this would undoubtedly be the last time they would see this gentlemen, most of the group took his picture one more time, while one or two of the more adventurous among them stood next to him so that they might be joined with him in photographic union. While he did not agree to this posing, neither did he resist. Indeed, all remarked how cheery he seemed to be while waving them a wordless farewell.

On their return to Chicago there was a tremendous rush by each and every one of the tourists to develop their films. All of them therefore realised at more or less the same time, all over the windy city, that there was no trace of the old Highlander in any of their snapshots.

Thank You and Goodbye

A Glasgow man always felt that his talents were unappreciated. For years he had slaved away at his desk with scant reward. Fed up with the ingratitude of his employers, he sought and secured a lucrative new job in the Far East.

He nevertheless continued to work hard for his Scottish employers, and they were delighted when he secured an exciting new contract for them with a first-time American client. In order to celebrate this new venture, a party was arranged at a plush city-centre bar. The occasion would also serve as a sending-off for the hard-working Glasgow man.

On the night everything went brilliantly. The just-flown-in Americans met everyone, while the Scots gave out the best of Caledonian hospitality. It only occurred to a very few that the man responsible for this deal was nowhere to be seen.

The next morning, as calls, faxes and e-mails arose, it became clear that there was no deal. The American's had been invited over to Scotland on a 'meet the people' visit – at the Scottish company's expense. The Scottish company had themselves been told that their new American customers would be paying for the night of expensive entertainment.

The only man who knew how this all came about was far, far away, already enjoying the brilliant sun of an Indonesian sky.

Forgotten Face

Two young sisters from Glasgow had borrowed their parents' car and caravan and were embarking on a tour of the Western Highlands. They took turns about driving and resting, as the glens and lochs of the land swept by them with unabashed grandeur. At night, the two would take advantage of whatever the local bar had to offer in terms of drink and men.

After one particularly hard night in a village pub, the younger sister demanded that she be allowed to sleep off her hangover in the caravan. Despite the laws of the road prohibiting such activity, the other sister agreed, seeing that her sibling was in need of a more intense rest than the front seat of the car could offer. A few hours later the older woman stopped for petrol. Woken by the jolt of the car stopping, the sleeping sister hopped out of the caravan and into the toilets adjacent to the petrol station, clad only in her turquoise pyjamas. Returning to the parked car a moment later, the older sister was soon on her way again, swerving gracefully out on to the open road.

It was some twenty miles further on that she became aware of a vehicle drawing alongside her. Alarmed, she turned to find the angry face of her younger sister, gesticulating wildly from the Land Rover of an amused-looking farmer.

Carluke Fertility Puzzle

A surge of births in Carluke was picked up by a visiting researcher at the local health authority. Unable to tell anything from the paperwork, the beady-eyed man scurried down to the town to see if anything could be discovered at first-hand.

Looking around the town, nothing seemed to be amiss. Having collected samples of tap water, the man seemed happy to be on his way. Then, as he was walking to his car, the ground seemed to rumble. Stopping, the researcher looked around and listened, catching the sound of a passing train. Getting out his files, the researcher then bought an *A–Z* of the town and set about checking the whereabouts of the railway line.

A few visits to some of the addresses that were part of the baby-boom phenomenon confirmed the clever man's suspicions, although it took a few embarrassing questions to complete the picture. The report to his superiors was succinct.

'Checks with the railway authorities confirm that, since approximately one year ago, heavy freight trains have been passing on the Carluke line in the early morning. Informal conversations with five of the couples involved have revealed that all of them had been wakened in the early morning by "some sort of rumbling" and, finding themselves awake together, they had indulged themselves with bed play. Hence the sudden increase in the birth rate.'

Technological Overload

A Scotsman from the farthest North was determined to travel the length and breadth of the USA, maximising his travel whilst minimising his costs. To this end, he flew to the East Coast and picked up a deluxe mobile home, of the type not normally seen on the roads of his homeland.

Impressed by its range of automated comforts, the man was soon heading north towards the famous autumnal colours of New England. One hour or so south of Boston, a police patrol car found the giant white road mobile lying in a ditch, motionless and with the power down. Not much later, the Scotsman was found lying concussed at the rear of the vehicle. Rushed to a nearby hospital, it was soon discovered that a slight bang to the head was the only damage.

Although his memory was sketchy at first, the cause of the accident was revealed in due course. Feeling the need for a drink and a snack, the traveller was looking around the control panel to find the right-hand indicator to show that he was about to pull over. While doing so he had found a switch marked 'cruise control'. Thinking that this was the equivalent of 'autopilot', the Scot had flipped the option to 'on', and then got out of the driver's seat and gone to make himself a cup of tea and a cheese toastie.

Road Pig Incident

A Dumfries man was visiting relatives in the far North. Not used to the winding roads and hills of the misty glens, he was taking particular care with his driving. On one road in the middle of apparent nowhere, the man was going along at a most gentle rate towards a blind corner. With a fantastic roar, an open-top sports car burst round the bend towards him on his side of the road, swerving as if out of control. The Dumfriesian just had time to slam on the brakes before the nifty little automobile sprang by him.

As it did so the young female driver turned towards him and shouted, 'Pig!'

Incensed, the man was able to shout, 'Stupid witch!' before the woman sped off.

Restarting his car, the man drove round the corner, still glaring with anger into his rear-view mirror. Thus, he did not see the large pig standing in the middle of the road before it was far, far too late.

Infidelity Gardener

A man in Elgin had a beautiful but flirtatious girlfriend. Although many spoke of her infidelity behind his back, none were willing to confront him with the truth, so complete and unquestioning was his love.

Just before departing on one of her occasional holidays to Ibiza, the lovely young lady became careless and left an envelope of recent party snaps lying around the apartment she shared with her gullible, doting boyfriend. Finding these on the evening before she flew out, the young man was beside himself with grief at her duplicity. That very night he moved out. Returning, the woman read his accusatory note and laughed it all off. So what if he had gone? At least now she had the place to herself for further adventures. Besides, she had her holiday to get on with.

It was only when she came back, a little browner, two weeks later that the naughty girlfriend realised that, far from simply moving out, her ex-boyfriend had sown every carpet in the house with alfalfa seeds. Opening the door, the woman was confronted by a green, fetid, rotting jungle.

Valuable Advice

Two American fishermen had long nurtured a dream of going to Scotland for a holiday combining the delights of golf, whisky and fishing. No expense was spared in pulling together the ultimate male getaway. This would be a trip that they could boast about for many years to come.

Arriving at Glasgow Airport, they were picked up by a luxurious Range Rover that whisked them to one of Edinburgh's top hotels. From there it was on to St Andrews and a round on the magnificent Old Course, before moving on through Gleneagles, Loch Lomond, Turnberry and then up to Nairn and other celebrated names in the realm of golf. Along the way they stopped at every distillery that they could, sampling the best of the Lowlands, Highlands and Islands produce, before coming to rest on Speyside, the centre of the malt whisky industry.

From a prestigious hotel in Craigellachie they plotted their next move. Adamant that they should make a huge catch, the pair inquired who was the best guide in the area.

'That'll be Jimmy the Ghillie,' was the unanimous response.

That night Jimmy was tracked down to a nearby pub, where he sat nursing a half pint of beer and a large nip of the local whisky. As he listened to the Americans' wishes, he nodded softly.

After they had finished making their explanation, Jimmy paused, before quoting them a cost for his services that was nearly equal to that of the entire holiday. Even the cash-rich Yanks were stunned by the humbly dressed old man's demands.

'Listen, buddy,' one of them noted with tart directness, 'anyone can take us to the Spey. Lots of people know how to cast a rod in these waters and hundreds of people know good places for fishing.'

'Aye, well, that might be right,' said Jimmy, 'but as I understand it, you've only got two days left. And unlike anybody else you might consult, I know *exactly* where to go and *exactly* what to do to *guarantee* a big catch.'

With that he downed his whisky and started for the door, pursued two minutes later by a couple of sheepish Americans who needed but a few moments to work out the correct value for a lifetime of experience.

Big Surprise

An Inverness woman came home unexpectedly one day and heard noises coming from her daughter's bedroom. Creeping up the carpeted stairs, the mother was shocked to discover that not only was her sole female child skipping school, but she was also enjoying sexual union with a boy from her class. Enraged, the woman gave them both a stern lecture on the dangers of unprotected sex, while also noting how such activity would do little for either of their chances of securing a place at university.

Initially silent, the feisty daughter tired of her mother's hectoring tones and explained that, firstly, she didn't want to become a doctor and secondly, 'There's no chance of me becoming pregnant.'

The mother was furious. 'How can you be so sure that you won't get pregnant, young lady?' she demanded, setting aside the question of a career in medicine.

The daughter then explained how she had been stealing her mother's own contraceptive pills for two months now, cutting tiny slits into the packaging and easing them out in a way which left the foil cover unharmed. The pills were then replaced with standard headache tablets.

The next week the mother discovered that she herself was expecting. Her daughter later became a lawyer.

Limp Joke

A top surgeon from Kilmarnock was enjoying the traditional stag night before the wedding. Having eaten well to ensure that he had a full stomach on which to nest the alcohol, he was keen not to allow any tomfoolery from his hospital colleagues to interfere with his wedding plans. Yet interfere they did, spiking drink after drink until he passed out. At this point someone suggested taking him to the infirmary for some additional japery.

Waking on his wedding morning in a hospital bed, the surgeon was furious to learn that, in a moment of highjinks, he had broken his leg. Looking down at the cast, under which lay a perfectly fine leg, he cursed his luck and set about getting ready for his marriage as best he could. His best man was on hand to help him get dressed, and together they drove round to his house and put on their respective wedding outfits. With a tremendous summation of dignity, the surgeon hobbled down the aisle on crutches, one white plastercast sticking out from his family kilt. At the reception, he did the best he could to dance, to the amusement of his so-called friends.

After both bride and groom had been driven off to the airport, the group of hospital chums decided that they could not take the joke any further. That night they telephoned his hotel in Mauritius to explain the joke, fearing his angry reaction even at a great distance. They need not have worried. Concerned that his friends might try some sort of trick on his honeymoon, the surgeon had lied about the hotel that he and his wife would be staying in. It was fully two weeks before he learned the dastardly truth.

Antique Morality Tale

A wily antiques dealer from the south side of Edinburgh would go on frequent tours of the Highlands, attempting to find rare pieces of furniture that the less-worldly country folk might not fully comprehend in value.

Walking through an old farmyard on his way out after a disappointing visit, the dealer noticed a cabinet nestling under a pile of old tractor tyres. Pulling one or two off, it soon became clear that this was a fine old Chippendale – dirty but otherwise in excellent condition. His wallet lit up in anticipation of a lucrative auction.

The farmer, noticing the interest his visitor was taking, approached and asked if the Edinburgh gent had found something interesting.

'Not really,' the dealer explained, 'but the legs are nice and would be good for a table I have back in the shop.'

After a spot of good-natured haggling, the farmer agreed on a price of a few pounds.

Smiling, the dealer set off to get his four-wheel drive hatchback, parked back on the mud track outside the farm.

Bringing the car to rest next to the pile of tyres, the dealer was in time to see the farmer administering a final axe blow to the pile of wood that had previously been a Chippendale cabinet. The dealer stumbled out of his expensive car, mouth wide open.

'I've done you the favour of chopping the rest of it up for firewood,' the farmer beamed. 'The legs you're after are over there.'

Inconsolable, the dealer picked up the legs, handed over the agreed sum, and took the long road back to Edinburgh, a journey on which there was ample time to consider on the importance of honesty.

Unknown Territory

A pleasant young man from Ayr was on his first ever trip to London, the result of winning a prize in a local raffle. Having been photographed at the bus terminal, the 19-year-old barely slept at all on the way South. Bleary-eyed, he stared out at the passing landscape of England, his spirit leaping with excitement at the imminence of a great adventure.

Arriving in the heaving city, the teenager checked into his central, if undistinguished, hotel before dashing out to take in the wonders of one of the world's major capitals. All day he trod the busy streets, agog at the people, places and prices. At night he wrote postcards.

On the second day of his trip, the young man undertook an extensive tour of the art galleries, running around each with the enthusiasm of a pup and delighted to find himself so deeply steeped in culture. That night he wrote more postcards.

The third day found the young man in some respects at odds with himself. He reflected at breakfast how, although he had been in this exciting city for over two days, he had not really met anybody. The millions of people around him were little more than animated figures in a world of which he was not a part. In order to fully participate he needed to meet people, to talk and exchange ideas with them.

So determined, the young man set about talking to those he found himself beside in cafés, on the street, outside shops. While most were somewhat sceptical of his friendly advances, by and by the 19-year-old felt that he was breaking through. As night fell he did not wish to stop.

Selecting a pub in the trendy Soho area, the boy from Ayr ordered a lager and sat himself at the bar. Before long he was in conversation with another man of similar age if not appearance, who invited the Ayrshire boy to join him and his companions at their table. Thrilled to become part of a crowd, the young man was soon accepted by all and stayed with this group when they left for a nearby club.

At this point, his memory becomes hazy. He remembers dancing and drinking and meeting many more people. He can recall going back to his hotel room with a girl who he met outside the club after it closed. He can still taste the sweetness of her perfume as they kissed on his bed. And he can remember waking on his duvet, alone in the dim light of an overcast London sky.

The girl was nowhere to be seen. But there was a note. Opening it, the young man hoped for a telephone number, and was disappointed to find the handwritten message, 'Welcome to The World of Aids'.

All Mod Cons

Computer help desks have come to fear the telephone call from Scotland. This one was no exception.

'It's about my computer.'

'Yes, sir?'

'There's something wrong with the coffee cup holder.'

'The coffee cup holder?'

'Aye. You see, every time I put my cup in it, the thing zooms back into the machine. There's coffee everywhere.'

'Where is this coffee cup holder, sir?'

The patient technician then listened as the man from Hamilton described his CD-ROM drive.

Brush Off

The western Highlands. A middle-aged English couple, eager to swap the fetid heat of competitive London for the rural peace of a slower place, have hired a luxurious camper-van and are driving around, sampling the best of Scottish scenery and hospitality.

Coming to rest one night in a particularly beautiful spot overlooking Loch Fyne, the couple set up their picnic table and begin to feast on some smoked salmon, washed down with a glass of smooth whisky. Their peace is disturbed by the sound of the local pipe band practising in a neighbouring field. This is more than the couple can stand. Incensed, the man strides over to the practising group of, mostly, young men and demands silence. Stunned, the kilted group comply. The man marches back to his wife and their idyllic enjoyment of fine Scottish fare continues in peace.

Following their meal, the couple decide to wander into the village to enjoy a pint or two of Scottish beer. On their way they notice the despondent group of pipers, now huddled together in conference on the grass. Coming back to their van a few hours later, the couple are alarmed to discover that someone appears to have been looking around their campsite. Checking that all is in order, they notice that the gang of pipers has now disappeared. Having ascertained that nothing is missing, the husband and wife decide to forget about it.

One week after returning to their high-powered jobs in London, the husband picks up the holiday photos they had taken on their Caledonian sojourn. There at the end are a couple of snapshots showing the band of pipers, with their kilts hiked up displaying the traditional lack of underwear, with what appear to be the couple's toothbrushes sticking out of an unexpected place.